INFORMATION SCIENCE

AN INTEGRATED VIEW

INFORMATION SCIENCE

AN INTEGRATED VIEW

Anthony Debons
Esther Horne
Scott Cronenweth

G. K. Hall & Co.
Boston • Massachusetts

INFORMATION SCIENCE:
AN INTEGRATED VIEW

ANTHONY DEBONS, ESTHER HORNE,
SCOTT CRONENWETH

Copyright 1988
by G.K. Hall & Co.
70 Lincoln Street
Boston, Massachusetts 02111

Library of Congress Cataloging-in-Publication Data

Debons, A.
     Information science : an integrated view / Anthony Debons,
Esther Horne, Scott Cronenweth.
        p. cm. -- (Professional librarian series)
     Includes index.
     ISBN 0-8161-1857-4. ISBN 0-8161-1877-9 (pbk.)
     1. Information science. I. Horne, Esther E. II.
Cronenweth, Scott. III. Title. IV. Series.
Z665.D43 1988
020--dc19
                    88-12666
                    CIP

Contents

Figures and Tables

Preface

The goal of this book is to provide a framework of concepts and issues that constitute a science of information as it relates to building information systems. It is intended for those who are unsure about what information science is. Information science is not just about computers and data processing. Information science is not just about the storage and retrieval of recorded knowledge. It is not just about cognitive psychology, or human information processing, or communication technology. These fields and many others all contribute to information science. Yet information science is more than the sum of these parts.

Information scientists have applied the conventional perspectives of the physical sciences to the study of information. A conceptual framework that integrates information technology with ideas about information as a phenomenon, however, has been by and large absent. This volume is an attempt to provide such a structure, albeit only one among a number of possible structures. The rationale for the structure of the book is based on two fundamental premises, premises that can be said to enjoy a certain degree of acceptance by those who consider themselves to be information scientists. The first premise is that information science is interdisciplinary in character. The second premise is that the objective of the science is the information system (although opinions may vary as to what an information system is). Interdisciplinarity and systems concepts are interrelated. Implicit in any systems concept is interdisciplinary synthesis, while interdisciplinary thinking inherently views phenomena from the systems perspective.

Convictions, perceptions, and attitudes about information science must be placed in the systems perspective. The systems perspective is simple: a system is an interrelated aggregation of parts directed toward an objective. The systems perspective is a way of thinking about all the parts of the system and their individual functions in light of the objective of the system as a whole. The systems perspective is a fundamental premise of this book.

Like any science, information science is shaped by political and social forces, and by individuals with varying motivations, interests, and predispositions. Many practitioners of information science were never formally educated in information science per se. They bring with them ways of dealing with problems from other scientific disciplines. The systems perspective provides the basis for synthesizing these varied approaches.

As Einstein said, "All theory is applied, and all applications lead to theory." Information science emerged out of a need to solve real world problems. It also has a broad theoretical base, however. This book attempts to organize the numerous theoretical and applied contributions of many scientists into a framework that can be applied, via the systems perspective, to building information systems that truly provide information. It is not possible to include the work of all the scholars and engineers who have contributed to information science. Those interested in finding out more about a topic, or in adding their own theoretical perspective to that which we present, are encouraged to study the bibliography at the end of each chapter. We do not (and cannot) attempt to provide a reference to every work relating to the subjects we cover. Rather, we have attempted to provide a framework upon which each individual must build.

Given that information science is the study of the laws and principles that govern information systems as defined, the task is to provide those interested in understanding the concept of information with the varying perspectives that relate directly to the term information. This is presented in Chapter 1. Chapter 2 attempts to describe those who direct their energies in the day-to-day problems of information as well as the challenge involved in its study--the information professional. Chapter 3 describes the tools that are available to the scholar and the practitioner in the study of both information as a basic phenomenon and the information system as the embodiment of the phenomenon in day-to-day environments. Chapter 4 details the major principles related to systems theory, which forms the fundamental construct of the science.

Chapters 5 and 6 provide an overall survey of the technologies that are included in information systems. In this connection, the reader is cautioned to note the important differences that exist between information and communication technologies. While information technologies augment human ability to *process* data (or signals), communication technologies are essentially technologies that *transport* signals. Although intimately related, they are grounded on different principles both ontologically and operationally. Chapter 7 discusses information system synthesis, which is fundamental to our objectives because it is intrinsically related to the premise of interdisciplinarity. If information systems consist of a number of constituent components (much like the human organism), what are the factors directly related to their integration? A synthesis is postulated on the proposition that organisms are information systems, and that the organism can serve as a metaphor to provide the basic framework for such systems. Based on this proposition, there are two interfaces in question: first, the interface that exists among components of a system and serves to provide system homeostasis for achieving objectives; second, the interface that exists between the human and the technology when the human serves as a component of a larger information system. Chapter 8 examines the impact of information systems, particularly on individual privacy. Again, it is cautioned that the impact of information systems and communication systems as they relate to each other may differ, and the difference may be critical to our ability to establish policy regarding each. Finally, Chapter 9 explores the future of information science.

The philosophy that this book represents is the result of over twenty years of research and often vehement debate. The authors hope it will aid others in the search for an understanding of that most elusive of phenomena--information.

The authors extend their warmest thanks to the thirty-four graduate students of the Department of Information Engineering, Jilin University of Technology, Changchun, People's Republic of China, for their indulgence during the harsh winter of 1985, allowing for the preparation of the initial manuscript and facilitating the exchange of ideas among the authors who were separated by many earthly miles. Grateful acknowledgment is also extended to Perry Ricker, V. Silverman, among others of the class of winter 1986, Interdisciplinary Department of Information Science, University of Pittsburgh, who examined the draft in detail. Last but certainly not least thanks to Arleen Girty, secretary, Interdisciplinary Department of Information Science, who labored over many difficult handwritten versions of the manuscript.

1
Perspective

Information is part of all human experience. Acquiring and processing information are fundamental aspects of life itself. Current interest in a "science" of information has developed as the result of the complexity of life's problems. The rapid development of technology, the growth of knowledge, and the fast pace of the modern world create an increasing awareness of the importance of information and the need for professionals dedicated to studying and understanding it.

In this chapter we will define what is meant by *information* and the phrase *information science*. We will sketch the development of information science and attempt to provide a basic understanding of it by looking at the interests and career paths of professionals identified as information scientists. Finally, we will outline other fields of study associated with information science and its objectives.

THE NATURE OF INFORMATION

The late scholar Fritz Machlup (1983) carefully assessed the different meanings associated with information. Some interpretations that have been made from these sources are as follows:

1

Something one did not know before.
A clue.
Something that affects what one already knows.
How data are interpreted.
Something useful in some way to the person receiving it.
Something used in decision making.
Something that reduces uncertainty.
The meaning of words in sentences.
Something that provides more than what is stated.
Something that changes what a person who receives it
       believes or expects.

Our understanding of the basic nature of information is clouded by the fact that the word is used in a variety of different contexts in our daily speech. The most prevalent of these everyday uses are discussed below.

Information as a Commodity. This refers to an item in a book, in someone's head, in a corporate file, or a statistic. When information is regarded as a commodity, it often assumes economic value. Management of the commodity becomes paramount. The meaning of the expression "information [or knowledge] is power" becomes obvious. If an individual or organization has sole possession of a particular body of information/knowledge, that information/knowledge may enable whoever holds it to achieve objectives. Information/knowledge can thus provide control over objects and persons.

Information as Energy. Those who view information as energy regard it as a quantifiable physical entity whose presence or absence can be verified experimentally. It can be argued that information is transmitted by, or embedded in, ordinary forms of energy. The information provided by sound waves emitted by a train whistle is one example of how it can be described in terms of energy.

Information as Communication. Information is often considered to be synonymous with communication. When one person is communicating with another, the person initiating the exchange of data is moving or transferring his or her understanding of the data (together with the actual data) to the other person (the receiver). When the data are received the person becomes

informed.   Being informed, therefore, is the result of
communication, or *information transfer.*   If we remove the
understanding of the data (its meaning) and only move the actual
data, we then have *data transmission,* the physical denoting or
movement of signals.

Information as Facts. Information is often thought to be the
same as fact. What is today's date? When is your birthday? How
much are your monthly wages? When the term information is used
in this way, it does not necessarily mean that there is any implied or
actual use of the fact, although one usually wonders about
birthdates, for example, for some purpose: to arrange a party, to
purchase a gift. Everyone possesses facts about events and objects
for which no direct need (at least at the moment) is suggested.
When given to you, a fact arouses your interest--you are aware, but
that is often the extent of your concern. Unless the fact is placed in
context, it remains just that--a fact and nothing else.

Information as Data. Information is often thought to be the
same as data. This may seem to reiterate the previous discussion
regarding information as fact, but the difference lies in the
definition of the words *fact* and *data.*   Data are the products of
symbols that are organized according to established rules and
conventions. For example, when you arrange letters and numbers
(symbols) in certain ways, these letters and numbers become data.
A fact is one or many data elements embedded in some context. A
fact has meaning. The symbols EVL495 are data. They could mean
anything or nothing. In the context of a vehicle registration form,
they become a license plate number--a fact. Thus, when we think of
information as synonymous with data, we mean that it may
sometimes be convenient for us to discuss information in the
absence of meaning or context.

Information as Knowledge.   Information is often used
interchangeably with knowledge. Knowledge implies a state of
understanding beyond awareness.   It represents an intellectual
capability to extrapolate beyond facts and draw original conclusions.
Knowledge must be deduced, not simply sensed. What we "know" or
"think" is often called "information."

DEFINITION OF IMPORTANT TERMS

As the definitions above point out, the word *information* can be applied to a continuum of cognitive states, from sensory awareness to synthesis of ideas. If we are to deal scientifically with ambiguous words such as data, information, and knowledge we need a more thorough understanding of what they mean. In defining such words we face problems inherent in the definition of all terms. One problem is that it is difficult to say what anything is, in terms that will stand up to rigorous tests of logic. Determining the basic nature of something requires considerable study and effort. Another difficulty concerns the problem of consensus: definitions based on consensus depend on agreement among those who use the term. Individual viewpoints and opinions can lead to great differences in how we view terminology.

In a review of the terminology of information science Trauth (1978) found that the twenty definitions she examined could be categorized into four groups of meaning. The first category stresses the external movement of the information itself. The second category proposes that information is a process-oriented concept in that movement from source to destination is internal to both sender and receiver. This implies that no physical change in state takes place. The third category views information as an object operating within some dynamic process, such as decision making or problem solving. The final category refers to information seen as fact or discrete data elements. This wide variety of perspectives illustrates that data, information, and knowledge are used quite differently depending on context and intention. At times the context and intention are not clear, or are in opposition to other equally valid contexts and intentions.

Another basic problem with the use of these words is that they can be used interchangeably. We often change the way we use the word depending on what we are thinking--our point of reference.

The Knowledge Spectrum

Data, information, knowledge, and wisdom can be viewed as part of a continuum, one leading into another, each the result of actions on the preceding, with no clear boundaries between them.

The knowledge spectrum is presented in figure 1.1. The *event* is an occurrence, some condition or change in the state of the world. This state or condition has to be represented if we humans are to deal with it. We invent *symbols*--numbers, letters, glyphs, or pictures become representations of the event. When we use rules to organize such representations, we generate a *datum* (singular) or *data* (plural). Both our number system and our language are such representations.

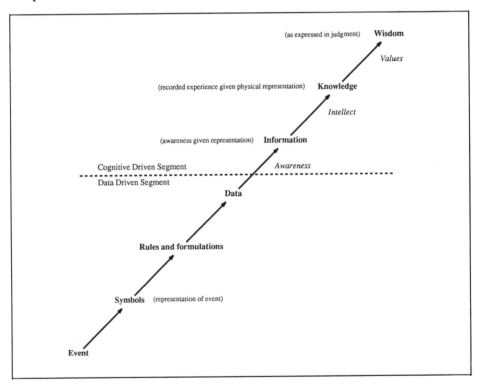

Figure 1.1. The Knowledge Spectrum.

We perceive data when they stimulate one or more of our senses. When we are exposed to these stimuli, we become *aware* (a state of consciousness) of data about the event. At this point, most of us say that we have acquired *information*. What we really mean is that we are now informed. Being informed means that we are aware of some occurrence, but nothing else. We can respond to this information in a number of ways: we can store it in our minds (we call this memory) or we can jot it down on a piece of paper. This physical or cognitive representation of data about which we are aware is *information*.

When we apply meaning or understanding to our awareness, higher cognitive processes are involved. When we apply such processes, we sense that we understand, and can apply what we understand to those things that require resolution. This understanding enables us to analyze situations and to put things into their proper perspective. It enables us to pass judgment on these situations and conditions and the facts that influence them. Thus, when we go beyond awareness (by our own intellectual actions), we can say that we have *knowledge*. Now we can do with knowledge what we did with information. Knowledge can be part of our thinking, our memory, our way of looking at the world. We can give our knowledge physical representation by packaging it in books, records, and the like. The ultimate step in the knowledge spectrum is *wisdom*, which always involves the inclusion of values in judgment.

If we have access to knowledge, we can build on it, applying values, ethics, and reason to what we know until we arrive at a conclusion that benefits and elevates ourselves and others. To elevate oneself and others through knowledge, values, ethics, and reason is to be wise. The productive output of the wise is wisdom. States beyond wisdom are perhaps more of the spirit than the mind, and so are outside the knowledge spectrum.

The transformations from data to information, knowledge, and wisdom can be represented as part of a spectrum of cognition that characterizes human competence in dealing with life's events. This spectrum is hierarchical. Each transformation (e.g., event to symbols, symbols to data, data to information) represents a step upward in human cognitive functioning.

An *information system* makes possible the transformation of data to information. A *knowledge system* is a greater system of which an information system is only a part. A knowledge system (see fig. 1.2) describes the transformations that take place within human social networks whose goal, stated or otherwise, is to increase the sum of human wisdom. For example, scientists in a given discipline derive data from theories and experiments, leading to information about specific events. By sharing this information in journals, conferences, and so forth, others become informed, and an understanding of a phenomenon emerges. This understanding eventually leads to greater knowledge of related events. At some point, it is hoped, humankind is wiser with respect to the universe of events of which we are a part.

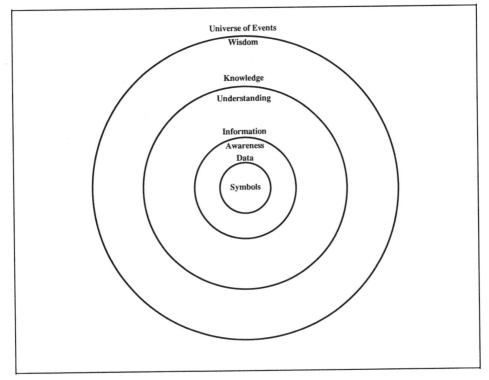

Figure 1.2. The Knowledge System.

It is because of the ambiguity of the terms implicit in the knowledge spectrum that standards for the use of terms seem desirable when attempting to develop professional skills specifically oriented to information and information systems.

Standardization of Terms

The following definitions round out our explanation of the concept of the knowledge *spectrum*. They also summarize the basic position and assumptions of the authors relative to the terminology that forms the foundation of the science of information. The meanings hold throughout the remainder of this text.

Data: Letters, numbers, lines, graphs, and symbols, etc., used to represent events and their state, organized according to formal rules and conventions.

Information: The cognitive state of awareness (as being informed) given representation in physical form (data). This physical representation facilitates the process of knowing.

Knowledge: The cognitive state beyond awareness. Knowledge implies an active involvement and understanding and the ability to extend the level of understanding to meet life's contingencies. Knowledge can also refer to the organized *record* of human experience given physical representation (books, reports).

Wisdom: Implies the application of knowledge as contained in human judgment centered around certain criteria or values that are generally accepted by the culture or society.

THE SCIENCE OF INFORMATION

Many professionals feel quite comfortable with their understanding and use of the phrase information science. Others feel that, because its subject matter is so difficult to come to terms with, nobody can say with authority what information science is really all about. Some argue that because it is a new field, lack of definition is desirable because it allows a greater range of thought to be developed. Without arguing the merits of these rationales, the authors see a need to present a framework upon which a study of information can proceed.

Our perception of the concept of information science is based on the assumption that all organisms are information systems. The need for awareness regarding the world is so important to survival that it forms the very basis of life. Through its sensory, cognitive, and motor components, the organismic information system transforms data into information which leads to a state of awareness of the environment. By extending the capacity to be aware (through the creation of artificial information systems), the ability of human beings to create, invent, and share ideas is extended.

The information system is an environment of persons, machines, and procedures that augment human biological potential to acquire, process, and act upon data. It thus improves our chances for survival.

The Development of Information Science

Humans have always been concerned with information and knowledge. Information science historically has many primary roots, one being epistemology, or the study of knowledge. In the modern sense, information scientists are primarily concerned with two basic fundamentals: the needs to *count and account* and to *record and communicate* (fig. 1.3).

Contemporary information science has its basis in three forces that emerged in the 1950s and have continued into the 1980s. In the early 1950s, the Scientific and Technical Information (STI) program provided government funds and momentum toward development of America's scientific knowledge base. It was a direct result of Sputnik and other Soviet technological advances. The STI provided the stimulus for the reexamination of how scientific material was propagated and disseminated. The European influence here was expressed in the so-called documentalist (and later bibliometrist) disciplines, which emphasized the need to develop scientific principles governing the storage and retrieval of information (Walker 1967).

Counting and Accounting	Recording and Communicating
clay tablets	speech
abacus	prehistoric art
first coins	cuneiform script
bookkeeping	calenders
paper money	early alphabets
adding machine	writing
calculating machines	libraries
automatic loom (Jacquard, 1801)	printing press (1450)
analytical engine (Babbage, 1833)	Library of Congress (1806)
mathematical logic (Boole, 1850)	telegraph (1837)
Hollerith cards	typewriter (1866)
Mark I (early computers)	telephone (1876)
Turing machine (1937)	phonograph (1877)
ENIAC computer (1944)	photography (1888)
stored programs (1947)	radio (1895)
microprocessors (1948)	films (1896)
UNIVAC computers (1954)	Shannon's Theory of Communication (1949)
time sharing computers (1960)	satellites (1958)
"third generation" computers	telecommunications
BASIC programming language	OCLC
"fourth generation" computers	early library automation
VLSI architectures	first information science departments
"fifth generation" computers	modern resource sharing networks

Figure 1.3. Historical Roots of Information Science. (From Augarten 1984.)

Another stimulus for the development of a science of information was the military program directed at developing information systems, called command-control-communication systems (C^3), to support the deployment of US military forces and firepower in the event of an attack on the United States. Every branch of the service initiated research programs, employing a wide spectrum of scientific disciplines in their development. An example of such a program is one developed at Hanscom Field outside Boston by MITRE Corporation in the early 1960s. In conjunction with the Air Force, MITRE developed a C^3 system to meet strategic and tactical requirements in response to the perceived Soviet ballistic missile threat. Earlier successes experienced by the military in the application of state-of-the-art computer technology to the control of missiles in the development of SAGE (semiautomated ground environment) provided the basis for the development of more sophisticated systems. The early work done by Newell and Simon at Carnegie Institute of Technology (now Carnegie-Mellon University) was part of this push. In an effort to solidify this increasingly important perspective, the first International Congress on Information System Science was conducted in Hot Springs, Virginia, in 1961. This conference attracted scholars from numerous fields providing the interdisciplinary character of an emerging science of information.

The growing realization by the government and the military of the power of computer technology soon spread to the industrial sector. Enormous amounts of research and development have been undertaken to apply existing information to the problems of managerial planning, operation, and control. In addition, these efforts are focused on developing information systems that can directly facilitate decision making, such as expert systems, decision support systems, and other forms of artificial intelligence.

The National Science Foundation has had a continuing interest in soliciting and supporting research relevant to information science. An important research arm of the government, the NSF responds to national needs and, through the Bureau of the Budget, acquires funds that are distributed to any source, academic or industrial, that can conduct research. Through its publications, the foundation is an important source in tracing the history and work of information science.

Several books have been published over the years that have made clear contributions to the development of the science of information. Eugene Garfield's (1977-80) three-volume account of events and thoughts characteristic of the early activities of information scientists provides an informal view of the field. The pioneering work of Hans Peter Luhan in the advancement of the automation of library functions provided the stimulus for formalizing documentation in the library. The later work of Kent, Perry, and others at Case Western in this aspect of information science was also based on the automation of the way we organize information for retrieval. Harold Borko's (1962) text provided an extended perspective on several subject areas that would ultimately represent the interests of information scientists. Tefko Saracevic (1970) provided the first basic framework of subject areas of interest to leaders in information science. In 1973 Joe Becker published an introductory text that identified the main interest of information science as information retrieval in the context of communication. Other significant works on the subject include Belver Griffiths (1980), C.H. Davis and James E. Rush (1980), and Donald King et al. (1978, 1983).

Interests of Information Scientists

If we cannot satisfactorily answer the question, "What is information science?" (at least not yet), we can certainly look at the problem from another point of view. If there is an information science, then there must be information scientists. What kinds of experiences (phenomena) do such people study? In chapter 2 we examine information professionals--not necessarily scientists, but persons who are educated and trained to perform tasks that depend in one way or another on what information scientists study and discover.

The work of information scientists is recorded in their experiments and studies and in their publications. Table 1.1 examines the subject areas of interest to those who claim professional identity within the field. These subject areas are reported in the *Journal of the American Society for Information Science*, the official publication of information scientists.

It is clear from this table that the major areas of interest of information scientists lie in the logistical (acquisition, storage, and retrieval) properties and requirements of knowledge.

The American Society for Information Science is not the only source of material of interest to information science professionals. Articles on the topics in table 1.1 can also be found in the journals of the following societies and professional groups, to name only a few: Association of Computing Machinery (ACM); Institute of Electrical and Electronic Engineers (IEEE); American Library Association (ALA); American Management Association (AMA); Association for Information and Image Management (AIIM); Society for Information Display (SID); Human Factors Society (HFS); and American Psychological Association (APA).

Perspective

Table 1.1. Subject Areas of Interest to Information Scientists by Category: Number of Citations per Year (JASIS 1979-86).

Category	1979	1980	1981	1982	1983	1984	1985	1986	Totals
Acquisition	1	1		2			1	1	6
Bibliometrics	1		1	3	1		3	1	10
Circulation	2								2
Citations		1	1	6	6		3	4	21
Classification	1	1							2
Cognition			2						2
Communications			2	1	1		1		5
Computers	2	2	4	1	2		1		12
Data base		1	3	2	1		1		8
Data files	2							1	3
Data transfer		1	1			1			3
Decision making				1			1		2
Distribution	1		1						2
Document retrieval	1	4					4	3	12
Education							3	1	3
Education and training	1	2		3					6
Electronic publishing							1		1
File maintenance	1					1			2
Human information processing			2						2
Indexing	3	2	3	3	2	1	2	1	17
Information (nature of)	11	2	7	11	4		1		36
Information and productivity							1		1
Information retrieval	2	2	4	2	4	1	2		17
Information science	4	1		5	3				13
Information seeking behavior					1	1	1		3
Information systems	3	2	4	1			2	1	13
Information technology (3rd world)							4		4
Information transfer							4		4
Knowledge	1						1		2
Library	5	3	5		3		3		19
Library information systems	1		1						2
Library networks	6					1			7
Literature	3	6	4	5	3				21
Manpower				1				1	2
Memory					1				1
Microfilm performance	1								1
Networks	6	1	1				1		9
Office Automation					5				5
Online		2	1						3
Online information systems		6							6
Online retrieval	1		2					1	4
Online searching	2	2	3	4	4	1	1	1	18
Online serials collections	2								2
Privacy		1							1
Research methods							4	1	5
Retrieval		1		3	2				6
Systems		1		6					7
Technology	1		2	1	3				7
User studies	1								1

One might gather from all this that the interests of information scientists are widely varied, and indeed they are; the concerns of information scientists are also of interest to psychologists, librarians, physicists, chemists, computer scientists, city planners, and others. Indeed, information science covers a wide range of scientific and engineering disciplines, as well as the humanities. Furthermore, many nations have exerted their efforts toward problems that center around information as a basic human resource. In our study ofinformation science we will discuss the content and direction of these efforts and thus be able to appreciate fully the international scope of the field.

The Boundaries of Information Science

There have been several attempts by information scientists to suggest a basic structure to the science. Among these, three conferences, in 1972, 1973, and 1978, were supported by the Scientific Affairs Division of the North Atlantic Treaty Organization (NATO). These conferences attended by international scholars provided the framework of one such structure in which the various interests and issues and knowledge of information scientists could be addressed. Papers presented at the conferences regarding the foundational aspects of information science included questions regarding definition of terms, the role of the various sciences comprising a science of information, methodologies to be applied in the study of information, and the possibility of generating paradigms in the organization of new science. Several areas were identified as inherent in or critical to the field.

Technology and Systems

Papers in the technology and systems area centered on the application of state-of-the-art technology to the needs of users of information, analysis and design of information systems, and evaluation of the efficiency and effectiveness of such systems and approaches to creating them.

Impact of Information Technology on Society

Contributors to this area of study examined the influences that technology has on individuals and organizations in societies and cultures across the globe. Problems of the information-rich and information-poor, the influence of new technologies in the practices of government, ideas for national information policies, matters of copyright protection, and issues of personal privacy and civil rights were brought up here.

Resources

The conferences included an assessment of human resources needed to sustain the activities of the science worldwide, the direction and extent of encouragement of research and development in the field, educational requirements and practices for the sciences, the role of practical training, and other related matters.

Foundational Disciplines

Many disciplines contribute to the science of information. Interdisciplinary sciences are applied sciences; they are pragmatic and problem-oriented, and require the synthesis of resources from many related areas. The four basic disciplines that are most important to the study of information are philosophy, mathematics (statistics), linguistics, and behavioral science.

Philosophy

The objective of philosophy is "to formulate a unified and consistent conception of the universe with the aim of understanding its ultimate nature" (English and English 1958). Philosophy's role in information science is twofold. First, it provides the rules of logic, which, when coupled with mathematical rules, enable the development of computing machines and concepts important in the development of modern information systems. Second, philosophy provides information science with an understanding of inquiry systems, the way individuals ask questions about the state of the world (Churchman 1971). Philosophy also provides the foundations of the social sciences that are relevant to the functioning of information systems.

Mathematics (Statistics)

Mathematics as a formal language enables one to quantify (measure) experience, which is an aim of all science. Mathematics, of course, is the foundation of statistics and other tools that information scientists use.

Linguistics

Linguistics, the study of language, is of particular interest to information scientists for two main reasons. First, language is an important tool in representing, classifying, and categorizing events. Second, and more important, language is a means for communication, which is the basis for all information and knowledge. Differences in culture and social practices may be reflected in fundamental differences in the representation of events, a critical matter to many information scientists as well as to linguists.

Behavioral Science

The behavioral sciences include all branches of psychology (social, cognitive, etc.) and sociology. In the final analysis, the most important part of any information system is the user, the person who generates, uses, and acts upon data, information, and knowledge. The principles that govern human behavior and our needs and wants for comfort and security, as well as our attitudes and our physiologies are critical to understanding any information system.

Related Fields of Study

Certain terms or phrases representing varying areas or fields of interest appear frequently in the information science literature. It is important to clarify their meanings and make their relation to information science explicit.

Informatics

The word *informatics* originated in the early 1960s, primarily in Europe and Japan. Although still used to some extent outside the United States to refer to information science, in most contexts it refers to the study of automation and automated technologies in document retrieval.

Information Engineering

The use of this expression in the literature is not consistent. For the Chinese, it refers to the application of Western information technology to the design and implementation of information systems to meet national objectives for industrial revitalization. It can also refer to various aspects of information system design.

Knowledge Engineering

This is a relatively new phrase, used primarily by those whose interests lie in artificial intelligence and expert systems. These topics are discussed later in this text.

Cybernetics

Cybernetics is the science of control. Related concerns include communications and system theory.

Bionics

Bionics attempts to apply an understanding of the function and characteristics of living systems to the development of biomechanical systems.

REFERENCES

Augarten, Stan. *Bit by Bit: An Illustrated History of Computers.* New York: Ticknor and Fields, 1984.

Becker, Joseph. *The First Book of Information Science.* Washington, D.C.: U.S. Atomic Energy Commission, Office of Information Sciences, 1973.

Borko, H., ed. *Computer Applications in the Behavioral Sciences.* Englewood Cliffs, N.J.: Prentice-Hall, 1962.

Churchman, C. West. *The Design of Inquiring Systems: Basic Concepts of Systems and Organization.* New York: Basic Books, 1971.

Davis, Charles H., and James E. Rush. *Guide to Information Science.* Westport, Conn.: Greenwood Press, 1980.

English, Horace B., and Ava Champney English. *A Comprehensive Dictionary of Psychological and Psychoanalytic Terms.* New York: Longmans, Green & Co., 1958.

Garfield, Eugene. *Essays of an Information Scientist.* Vols. 1-3. Philadelphia: ISI Press, 1977, 1979, 1980.

Griffith, Belver C., ed. *Key Papers in Information Science.* White Plains, N.Y.: Knowledge Industry Publications, 1980.

King, Donald W., ed. *Key Papers in the Design and Evaluation of Information Systems.* White Plains, N.Y.: Knowledge Industry Publications, 1978.

King, Donald W., et al., eds. *Key Papers in the Economics of Information.* White Plains. N.Y.: Knowledge Industry Publications, 1983.

Machlup, Fritz, and Una Mansfield, eds. *The Study of Information: Interdisciplinary Messages*. New York: John Wiley & Sons, 1983.

Saracevic, Tefko, ed. *Introduction to Information Science*. New York: R.R. Bowker, 1970.

Taylor, Robert S. *Value-Added Processes in Information Systems*. Norwood, N.J.: Ablex Publishing Corp., 1986.

Trauth, Eileen More. "A Study of Some of the Terms Relevant to the Field of Information Science." Unpublished collection of papers, Interdisciplinary Department of Information Science, University of Pittsburgh, 1978.

Walker, Donald, ed. "Information Science and Technology." Papers prepared for the Third Congress of Information System Science, MITRE Corp., Boston, Mass., 1967.

2
The Information Professional

It is not clear exactly when the phrase *information professional* was first used. It is certainly of recent origin, having begun to gain acceptance in the late 1960s. The concept of an information professional was popularized by the American Society for Information Science during the 1970s, a period of growing awareness of the importance of information to the international community.

Any attempt to understand what is meant by information professional must include a number of considerations:

1. What is meant by a "professional"?

2. Who is and who is not an information professional? How many are there in the job categories identified? Where are they employed? What kind of work do they do?

3. What kinds of skills do they bring to their jobs?

4. Where are they educated?

5. What elements of modern society make their work necessary or important?

What Is a Professional?

A professional career implies activity requiring an education at or above the baccalaureate level. Such activity is guided by certain standards. Professionals adhere to standards that may be self-imposed, or be established by a community of individuals who share common theoretical and technical interests and who agree on their own ethics. Professionals usually view themselves as such, implying commitment to excellence and adherence to the ethics of the profession.

Identification of Information Professionals

In studies aimed at identifying information professionals, investigators have had to provide their own definitions of various job titles and establish professional categories as frames of reference.

In 1972 the University of Pittsburgh conducted a study of approximately 3,000 industrial, academic, and governmental institutions nationwide for the purpose of determining the number of individuals who fell within four professional categories as developed by Shirey, Gupta, and Debons (1974).

1. Information theorists/scientists who are concerned with the laws, theories, philosophy, sociology, etc., of information science.

2. Information systems specialists who analyze information problems and design systems or networks to solve them.

3. Information intermediaries who work between the decision maker and the body of knowledge.

4. Information technologists who operate, maintain, and control information systems, consisting of individuals, acquisition, transmission and processing technologies, and related working procedures.

In a later study (Debons 1981) conducted by the same university, two categories were added:

1. Managers of information, who plan, develop, coordinate, and control information programs and the human and material resources needed for their implementation.

2. Educators and trainers of information workers, who provide education and/or training for all categories of information professionals, as well as paraprofessionals and nonprofessional information workers.

For the purposes of the 1981 occupational survey, the following criterion was used to differentiate the information professional from other closely related professional groups:

> An information professional may be differentiated from other professionals who may also work with data by the fact that s/he is concerned with the transfer of content and therefore with the cognitive intellectual operations performed on the data by the end user. (Debons et al. 1981)

This description stresses that the information professional is concerned primarily with *users* of information, and secondarily with logistics of handling (acquiring, storing, retrieving) material that has the potential for informing individuals. With this description as a framework for analysis, the survey yielded some important statistics on the relative numbers of information professionals. For example, in 1980 there were approximately 1.64 million information professionals working in nine specified categories in the United States (see table 2.1). In a corresponding study (Svenonius and Witthus 1981), it was estimated that over half the United States labor force are information workers.

Of the various categories under the heading "functions performed," the principal jobs of the 1.64 million information professionals were systems analysis and design; management of information operations, programs, services, or data bases; and other operational information functions. The total number of persons in these three categories amounted to roughly one-half the total number of information professionals covered by the survey.

INFORMATION FUNCTIONS	Number of Information Professionals	Standard Error	Proportion of Information Professionals (%)
Management of information operations, etc.	273,900	26,100	17%
Data/information preparation for others	213,500	36,800	13%
Data/information analysis for others	257,100	35,300	15%
Searching on behalf of others	92,000	10,000	6%
Remaining operational information functions	272,700	112,800	17%
Information systems analysis	265,800	60,600	16%
Information systems design	103,400	25,100	6%
Information research and development	20,700	6,900	1%
Educating/training information workers	42,800	7,300	3%
Other information functions	5,700	2,600	1%
Function not specified	93,400	42,700	6%
Totals	1,641,000	224,000	100%*

Table 2.1. Number of Information Professionals by Their Primary Information Function Performed (1980). (From Debons et al. 1981.)

Much of the training of these professionals was conducted in the private sector. Of those involved in educating and training information workers, more than six times as many were in industry and government rather than at colleges and universities. This imbalance can be attributed directly to industry's competitive nature, necessitating enormous investment in information resources for marketing, finance, accounting, strategic planning, production control, and other managerial and decision support functions. Almost half of all of the professionals work in industry, the government, and education. The remainder are evenly spread out among the major functions of management support, research, information services (nonlibrary), and finance.

According to the survey, about 22 percent of information professionals in this country are employed by state and local governments. Of these only about 12 percent work with computers.

About 29 percent work in education and training, 19 percent in libraries, 15 percent in information services of one kind or another, and 10 percent in management support. The remainder hold a variety of titles too numerous to mention here. Roughly one third of the total information professionals in state and local governments are classified as managers.

It is surprising that federal agencies employ only about 5 percent of all information professionals. About half work primarily with computers, 15 percent with management support, 18 percent with information services (nonlibrary), and 8 percent each in research and library work.

Only about 2 percent of all those in the sample are employed by colleges and universities. These include librarians, educational and training personnel, and computer personnel (one in four). The rest are divided among research, technical publications, statistical analysis, management support, and finance. Education is the only area in which librarians and learning resource personnel achieve numerical parity with other kinds of information professionals.

This survey yielded some important implications about who information professionals are and what sets them apart as an occupational subgroup. For example, although they work in a variety of organizational contexts and use all kinds of technologies, they have in common "concerns associated with the concepts basic to information flow within the general systems paradigm: input, processing, output, memory, small or large systems or subsystems, and so on." This general systems paradigm is seen as common among information professionals, which could be used in education, resource integration, and standardization of occupational classifications. The general systems paradigm could help information professionals develop career mobility, serving to help categorize and understand the information profession.

No consideration of the information professional would be complete without including the pioneer work done in 1978 by Fritz Machlup and his colleague Stephen Kagan from Princeton University. In introducing their work, it should be emphasized that they were essentially referring to a subset of the community of information professionals, namely, the communicators. In Chapter 1 we stressed that some scholars of information science consider information/knowledge to be the cognitive process that persons perform based on the data they acquire, while others consider it to be the commodity itself. According to Machlup and Kagan, the stress is on *communication* or the transporting of *packages of knowledge* (commodities). (Machlup and Kagan did not identify nor did they deny these categories of "information professionals.") These authors attempted to describe the *knowledge-producing* labor force and not those who deal with the theoretical and practical aspects implied by the word information. In 1980 Machlup further expanded on the role of communications by establishing the following categories:

1. A *transporter* of knowledge is one who delivers what he receives without changing it in the least (e.g., a mailman acts as a link in the chain of communication but does not modify what is received, transported, and communicated in any way).

2. A *transformer* of knowledge changes the form of a message but not its content (e.g., a secretary taking dictation and producing a business letter fits this description, as does a cryptoanalyst).

3. A *routine processor* of knowledge who changes both the form and the content of the message received (e.g., a bookkeeper).

4. A *discretionary processor* of knowledge is very like a routine processor, except that the person must make judgments in choosing what rules or procedures to follow in modifying a given message. Decisions involved in inventory evaluation are examples of this type of knowledge.

5. A *managerial processor* of knowledge receives a variety of messages and generates extracts, summaries, and so forth based on them. This individual also receives messages in the form of instructions from others higher up in the organizational hierarchy. Based on these, the managerial

processor will change the form and content of messages to whatever extent is deemed necessary.

6. An *interpreter* of knowledge changes both form and content of messages received, but must do so in a way that preserves as accurately as possible their essential meaning. Language translators are an obvious example.

7. An *analyzer* of messages received, in contrast to the interpreter, may use judgment, craft, and skill to such an extent that the message communicated may bear little or no resemblance to the message received (e.g., intelligence agent, historian).

8. An *original creator* of knowledge gathers a variety of input from numerous sources and, based on personal creativity and other attributes, communicates a synthesis of collective messages that is wholly different from any one message. Poets, novelists, and such fall into this category.

The number of individuals in the labor force represented in these various categories has changed considerably with the changing times. Porat (1977) found the growth of knowledge-producing work in the United States between 1940 and 1970 to be "dramatic," representing 43.1 percent of all labor effort in 1970, compared to 31.5 percent in 1940. The fastest growth occurred among interpreters, analyzers, and original creators. Discretionary processors and managerial processors experienced lower growth rates, mainly because of the growth of computer technology and automation in general. Numbers of transporters, transformers, and routine processors have grown fairly rapidly, mainly as a result of new job categories in information processing that have evolved in conjunction with new techniques in computation, instrumentation, and communication (Machlup 1980).

Education of Information Professionals

Library and information scientists have long attempted to determine the education that would best prepare the individual for work in the profession. Garfield (1980) referred to information science education as "an ivory tower of Babel."

For library scientists, educational criteria that would establish the graduate from a school of library science or librarianship has been guided by practice and to some extent by the accreditation philosophy of professional associations (ALA, SLA, etc.). The education of information scientists is a different matter. Because it is a relatively new field, guidelines for an educational program are not readily available. The early academic programs were amalgamations of courses in librarianship with a scattering of others, the content of which reflected what some believed to be the technical issues of the times, namely, information storage and retrieval, documentation, and bits and pieces of subjects related to automation and technology.

Paul Wasserman (1975), a pioneer in the study of manpower and educational requirements, conducted several studies providing some framework for an educational program in information science. The early work conducted in the 1960s and the 1970s attempted to identify courses that were conducted at that time at the various graduate schools in the United States. In Great Britain, the work of Herbert Schur and W. L. Sanders (1968) also focused on the educational and training of individuals who would be engaged in "technological library and information work."

The world's first designated graduate degree program in information science was established in 1963 at the School of Information and Computer Science at the Georgia Institute of Technology (Slamecka and Gehl 1978). An undergraduate program at the institution was established in 1972. These programs were predicated on the school's extensive research in theory of computations, theory of systems, cognitive processes, management, and general foundations of information science.

In 1967 the University of Dayton established an autonomous department of information science. The program at the graduate (MS) level structured its subject matter along four major core areas:

1. *Behavioral science*, to provide an understanding of human limits and capacities for data processing and information formulations.

2. *Basic science*, to provide the formal analytical tools required to approach a problem and its solution.

3. *Systems and technology*, to provide an understanding of the capacities and limitations of the state of the art in technology in the development of information environments.

4. *Computer science*, to provide a particular appreciation of the use of computers in human problem solving and, directly, in the use of computers for research projects.

In 1969, a group at the University of Pittsburgh, supported by the National Science Foundation, initiated an intensive study of an information science curriculum leading to a four-year program report on the subject. The study indicated that in 1972 eleven clusters would "define the information field" (Belzer et al. 1975). These clusters were identified as foundations of information science, theory of organization of knowledge, theory of computing, computer models, data processing, automation of library systems, management in libraries, system evaluation, behavioral aspects, statistics, and mathematics.

The clusters suggested that graduates would have knowledge in the following areas: technology, theory of organization, mathematics, language and linguistics, basic sciences, and management theory.

Tefko Saracevic (1983) of the Mathew A. Baxter School of Information and Library Science, Case Western Reserve University, also saw the curriculum structure as encompassing four major core areas as indicated in table 2.2.

	Core	Distributive Requirements
Information Area		
Resources	Structure, contents, types, searching and evaluation of print and computerized information resources	Information resources specific to various subjects; principles of information transfer
Organization	Structure, principles and methods of intellectual organization of information	Advanced principles in subject analysis; specialized applications, computer use
Management Area	Basic principles of effective management; applications in operations of libraries and information systems; collection development; library automation	Management of specific types of information services; user and effectiveness studies; marketing of libraries and information services
Technology Area	Present and anticipated technologies affecting libraries and information systems, their operations, and services	Fundamentals of information processing; advanced applications in libraries and information systems

Table 2.2. Curriculum Structure and Contents--Overview. (From Saracevic 1983. Reprinted with permission.)

M. L. Blake (1985) of the Department of Information Science, Strathclyde Business School, University of Strathclyde, Glasgow, outlined the following core areas for an undergraduate program in information science:

Fundamentals of information science

Theories of information
Concepts related to information
Theory and fundamental structures of materials for
information science
Theory and fundamental process of materials in information
science

Essential processes in information science

> Creation of information
> Recording of information
> Analysis and synthesis of information
> Storage of information
> Selection of information
> Queries for information
> Users and uses of information
> Dissemination of information
> Communication of information

Information technologies (IT)

> Tooling in information science and applications
> Networks
> Artificial intelligence
> Robot-human interaction
> Convergent technologies

Information work, general

> Information societies
> Human information systems

Information work, particular

> Shells of information work
> Career modes

While many professional information science educators seem to feel that very little consensus exists as to what constitutes an information science curriculum, the above collection of diverse examples suggests otherwise. Information science is not so nebulous that it cannot be taught. Indeed, many existing and proposed curricula provide an excellent educational base. As the above curricula suggest, information science is not just computer science or library science.

More recently, those interested in education for information science have moved in a different direction from those seeking courses to be included in academic programs. The search is now for competencies, that is, capabilities to perform tasks relevant to employment rather than the completion of formal academic courses. Very often these competencies or capabilities approximate characteristics of the individual rather than course curricula per se. For example, the following competencies have been identified (Flynn and Shirey 1983):

> Understanding of principles, facts, concepts, and procedures; problem solving by the principles of information transfer; appreciation of the social role of the profession; knowledge of client's (user's) capacity to establish systemic relationships; self-understanding and self-reliance; critical attitudes toward the profession's rationale and tools/technologies; continued professional growth; and identification and use of ethical principles.

There is continuing interest in identifying competencies for the library and information science fields. One study (Griffiths and King 1984) identified several types of knowledge considered critical to information work:

> *Basic knowledge* in such areas as language, communication, arithmetic operations.
>
> *Subject knowledge* of primary subject fields of users served, such as medicine, chemistry, law.
>
> *Library and information science knowledge*, such as the definition, structure, and format of information.
>
> *Knowledge about information work environments*, such as the information community, its participants, and their social, economic, and technical interrelationships.
>
> *Knowledge of what work is done*, such as that required to provide services and produce products.

Knowledge of how to do work, such as how to perform various activities, apply techniques, use materials and technology.

Knowledge of the organization or user community served, such as mission, goals, and objectives, user's information needs and requirements.

The same study identified the following skills: *basic skills* such as cognitive, communication, analytical, etc.; *skills related to each specific activity* being performed, such as negotiation of reference questions, evaluation of research; and *others* such as managing time effectively, budgeting, and making projections. Attitudes were also identified: *dispositional attitudes* toward one's profession, the organization served, one's work organization, and other persons such as users and co-workers; *personality traits/qualities*, such as confidence, inquisitiveness, sense of ethics, tenacity, etc.; and *attitudes related to job/work organization*, such as willingness to accept responsibility, willingness to learn, and desire to grow.

Academic Disciplines of Information Professionals

Because an information professional can participate in a wide range of related occupations, it is difficult to identify the role of job experience and other factors in developing the individual's skills, competencies, and attitudes. Furthermore, as well as can be determined, no study of the educational backgrounds of information professionals has yet been conducted. It can be inferred that the following disciplines are, in whole or in part, included in the education of information professionals.

Computer Science

Basically, academic computer science programs are focused on computer programming, logic, and mathematical problem solving. Reference is often made to information processing, but the term data processing is often more correct. Criteria such as user needs analysis and a global view of the definition of the problem that an application is created to solve may be of secondary importance.

Library Science

Education in library science centers primarily on librarianship. Librarianship is directly focused on the institution of the library and the services provided to the community. Library science concerns the principles that govern the acquisition, storage, and retrieval of knowledge. The following statement makes clear the point:

> Since any science concerns itself only with knowledge, library science in particular can embrace only one side of the fundamental phenomenon of librarianship which is transmission of the accumulated experience of society to its individual members through the instrumentality of the book. (Pierce and Burks, cited in Shera 1972)

Communication Science

Communication science deals with the principles that govern the handling of *messages* under varying conditions and capabilities. The focus of specific academic departments in this science varies from the engineering of media to the use of media in the home, to the structure and function of natural language, to advertisement and film presentation. Thus, although communication science is certainly interested in disseminating knowledge, thereby aiding in its creation and use, it mainly focuses on the means for doing so (Lin 1977).

Information Science

Given the debate surrounding the very existence of a science of information per se, it seems sufficient here to stress that the focus of information science programs in general is to provide individuals with an understanding of the principles that govern the acquisition, storage, and retrieval of knowledge. In this sense, information science complements library science education. Differences between the two, however, could be considered important, in that they reflect the backgrounds of the respective faculties and general orientation of the schools, colleges, or universities where the departments are housed. Some information science programs attempt to identify themselves with the information system, its analysis and design; others focus on the human information processing aspects; others directly on data processing systems; and others on knowledge resource sharing.

Engineering

Much of what information professionals do involves the use of technology. The genesis of much of the technology of information and communications systems emerged from research and development conducted by electrical and electronics engineers.

Business

Business schools have come to acknowledge the role and importance of information systems and decision support systems for management operations. Planning and controlling the activities associated with institutions are clearly dependent on information. The academic programs (as reflected in the texts that have been developed to support the courses that are offered) are largely concerned with data processing, particularly as to records management and related applications.

Interdisciplinarity and the Information Professional

As we have seen, attention to and interest in information as a phenomenon come from a wide variety of disciplines. Thus, information professionals make use of numerous processes and analytical techniques from other fields. For example, the statistical methods used by psychologists for the study of learning are modified by educators in the study of classroom performance and by information scientists to measure effectiveness of information transfer. The interdisciplinary approach attends to differences and similarities of the methods used and how they can be applied to problems common to several disciplines.

Interdisciplinarity is a way of looking at problems that emphasizes the role of the generalist in guiding specialists toward a solution ("Interdisciplinarity" 1972). While recognizing the importance of the general perspective, interdisciplinary thinkers understand that specifics are just as important, and that one should approach the expert in the specific area (the specialist) to contribute an approach and solution to the problem. The interdisciplinarian is an expert, not in specifics, but in *relationships* among specifics. This expertness in relationships means the following (Sherif and Sherif 1969):

1. The ability to understand the methods used by the various specific disciplines and how they are applied.

2. The ability to understand the conceptual language of the discipline--the formal ways of looking at problems that are directed at specific issues of that discipline.

3. The ability to extend and interpolate the methods of the various disciplines to the particular problems that cut across a number of disciplines.

Information professionals have to bring findings and perceptions of a number of areas to the problems they face. Computer science, communication science, library science, and information science are interdisciplinary because they are concerned with applied and practical problems and need all the knowledge resources available (from whatever field of interest) to resolve them.

The Information Infrastructure

The information infrastructure (El-Hadidy and Horne 1984) is made up of all the basic facilities and services upon which most of us depend. Just think of the consequences that result from a newspaper strike, a mail delivery stoppage, a television-radio blackout. All of these activities are part of that vast body of

36

resources that directly deals with information--that element that keeps us *aware* of what is going on, what has happened, and what could happen.

Information, like any other resource, requires control. Over the years the amount of paperwork both inside and outside of government has grown to staggering proportions. One of the special agencies of the government, the Commission on Federal Paperwork, was established to deal with policies and practices regarding the gathering, processing, dissemination, management, and control of information. Its goal was to reduce the unprecedented paperwork burden on businesses, individuals, and state and local governments. The commission accepted the fact that individuals and institutions in general failed to treat information as a valuable national resource and to manage it accordingly. The report of the commission (1977) described the information management infrastructure in nine professional identities: computers and associated automation technologies; data accounting, statistics, and actuarial analysis; communication and telecommunication; publishing, printing, and replication; libraries and library science; microfilm and miniaturization technologies; systems and management science; the information sciences; and the information arts.

Each of these groups has either as a goal or as a side effect of its work the advancement of our capability to collect, process, store, use, and disseminate data and information more effectively and efficiently. Unfortunately, however, there is a lack of coordination among these professional identities. Recently, some large organizations have established upper-level managers responsible for controlling the information resources of the organization. This individual is often called the *information manager* or *information resource manager* (Horton 1983).

The Invisible College

Another way we can consider the information professional infrastructure is to include the means that support the professional work that such individuals undertake. Of course, there are numerous outlets through which information professionals can associate with each other (often referred to as the "invisible college"), primarily composed of professional associations and journals (Crane 1972). Some of the organizations that deal in one way or another with information management and particularly with information resources are listed below.

Associated Information Managers (AIM)
316 Pennsylvania Avenue, S.E.,
Suite 400, Washington, DC 20003
(202) 555-1969

Association for Federal Information
Resources Management (AFFIRM)
c/o Woody Horton, 500 23rd Street
N.W., Apt. B901
Washington, DC 20037
(202) 293-5519

Association for Systems Management (ASM)
24587 Bagley Road
Cleveland, OH 42138

Association of Records Managers and
    Administrators, Inc., (ARMA)
4200 Somerset Drive, Suite 215
Prairie Village, KS 66208

Society for Management Information
    Systems (SMIS)
111 East Wacker Drive, Suite 600,
Chicago, IL 60601

There are also organizations with broader scope that implicitly address not only information resources management, but other information professionals. Some of these are:

American Management Association (AMA)
135 West 50th Street
New York, NY 10020
(212) 586-8100

American Society for Information Science
   (ASIS)
1010 16th Street, N.W.
Washington, DC 20036
(202) 659-3644

Association for Computing Machinery (ACM)
c/o Boulton Miller
Southern Illinois University at
   Edwardsville
School of Business
Edwardsville, IL 62025
(618) 692-2504

International Federation for Information
   Processing
Applied Information Processing Group
c/o Edgar Sibley
Alpha Omega Group
8121 Georgia Avenue, Suite 406
Silver Spring, MD 20910

Institute for Certified Records Managers (ICRM)
P.O. Box 89
Washington, DC 20044

Special Libraries Association (SLA)
1700 Eighteenth St., NW
Washington, DC 20009

American Library Association
50 East Huron St.
Chicago, IL 60611

The needs of information professionals are also addressed through trade journals and technical publications. Some journals dealing in whole or in part with information records management and frequency of publication are as follows: *ARMA Records Management Quarterly*; *Bulletin of the American Society for Information Science* (monthly); *Computerworld* (weekly);

Information Science (monthly); *Computerworld* (weekly); *Information Management* (monthly); *Information and Records Management* (monthly); *Information Services and Use* (monthly); *Infosystems* (monthly); *Journal of Systems Management* (monthly); *MIS Quarterly*; and *Special Libraries* (monthly).

REFERENCES

Belzer, Jack, James Williams, John Kronenbusch, and A.B. Gupta. "Curricula in Information Science: Four Year Progress Report." *JASIS* 26 (1975):17-32.

Blake, M.L. "Generic Elements in an Undergraduate Course in Information Study." *Journal of Information Science: Principles and Practice* 11, no. 1 (1985):19-26.

Crane, D. *Invisible Colleges: Diffusion of Knowledge in Scientific Communities*. Chicago: University of Chicago Press, 1972.

Debons, A., Donald W. King, Una Mansfield, and Donald Shirey. *The Information Professional: A Survey of an Emerging Field*. New York: Marcel Dekker, 1981.

El-Hadidy, B., and E. Horne. *The Infrastructure of an Information Society*. New York: North-Holland, 1984.

Flynn, Roger, and Donald L. Shirey. "Towards a Paradigm for Education in Information Science." In *Information Science in Action: System Design*, edited by A. Debons and Arvid Larson. Boston: Martinus Nijhoff Publishers, 1983.

Garfield, Eugene. "Information Science Education: An Ivory Tower of Babel. *Current Contents* 22 (1980).

Griffiths, Jose-Marie, and Donald W. King. "Educating the Information Professional of the Future." *Challenges to an Information Society*, Proceedings of the 47th ASIS Annual Meeting, Vol. 21. White Plains, N.Y.: Knowledge Industry Publications, 1984, 68-73.

Horton, Forest Woody, Jr. "The Emerging Information Manager Professional." In *Information Science in Action: System Design*, edited by A. Debons and Arvid Larson. Boston: Martinus Nijhoff Publishers, 1983.

"Interdisciplinarity: Problems of Teaching and Research in Universities." Center for Educational Research and Innovation (CERI). Paris: OECD, 1972, 25-26.

Lin, Nan. *The Study of Human Communications.* Indianapolis: Bobbs-Merrill Education Publishers, 1977, 32.

Machlup, Fritz. *Knowledge and Knowledge Production.* Volume 1 of *Knowledge: Its Creation, Distribution, and Economic Significance.* Princeton, N.J.: Princeton University Press, 1980.

Machlup, Fritz, and Stephen Kagan, "The Changing Structure of the Knowledge-Producing Labor Force." Discussion Paper Series, New York University, Center for Applied Economics. Paper no. 78-01, January 1978.

Porat, Marc Uri. *The Information Economy; Definitions and Measurements.* Washington, D.C.: U.S. Department of Commerce, Office of Telecommunications, 1977.

A Report of the Commission on Federal Paperwork. *Final Summary Report*, 3 October 1977. U.S. Government Printing Office, GPO stock number 052-003-00439-9.

Saracevic, Tefko. "Curriculum Revision in Information and Library Science." *Education* no. 1 (1983):318-34.

Schur, Herbert, and W. L. Sanders. *Education and Training for Scientific and Technical Library and Information Work.* London: Her Majesty's Stationery Office, 1968.

Shera, Jesse Hauk. *The Foundation of Education for Librarianship.* New York: John Wiley & Sons, 1972.

Sherif, M., and Carolyn W. Sherif. *Interdisciplinary Relationships in the Social Sciences.* Chicago: Aldine Publishing Co., 1969, 3-20.

Shirey, Donald L., Armand B. Gupta, and Anthony Debons. "The Future Market for Professionals in Information." In *Information Science: Search for Identity*, edited by Anthony

Debons. Proceedings of the 1972 NATO Advanced Study Institute in Information Science. New York: Marcel Dekker, 1974.

Slamecka, Vladimir, and John Gehl, eds. *Information Sciences at Georgia Institute of Technology: The Formative Years, 1963-1978*. Oxford: Pergammon Press, 1978.

Svenonius, Elaine, and Rutherford Witthus. "Information Science as a Profession." *Annual Review of Information Science and Technology (ARIST)* 16 (1981):307.

Wasserman, Paul. "International Educational Patterns in Information Science: Characteristics and Issues." American Society for Information Science, 38th Annual Meeting, Boston. *Proceedings 12, Information Revolution*, part 1. Edited by Charles W. Husbands. Washington, D.C.: American Society for Information Science, 1975.

3
Methods in Information Science

This chapter provides a general framework within which we can begin to understand how the information professional undertakes the tasks that are critical to his or her area of interest. It is beyond the scope of this work to discuss all the design and decision-making techniques used by information professionals in their work. Such techniques range from case-study explorations based on planned or unplanned observation to highly detailed research following accepted standards of study.

Chapter 1 examined areas of concern to the information professional, from information storage and retrieval to artificial intelligence. One way we can examine the methods used across this rather broad spectrum of interest is to organize our thinking within a conceptual framework, which can help us understand how new knowledge in the field is gathered and correlated.

THEORETICAL AND APPLIED METHODS

We can begin by making an important distinction between those studies that attempt to understand the phenomenon (or experience) in question and those that attempt to address problems that have arisen in the field and require solution. The words *theoretical* and *applied* have been used to describe these distinctions, which is rather artificial, because most areas represent a marriage of both theoretical and applied considerations.

As we found in chapter 2, a wide range of functions, roles, and identities is subsumed by the phrase information professional. The methodologies applied across such a range are similarly broad and diverse. The classic methods used in inquiry and investigation are derived from Ptolemy, Aristotle, Plato, Bacon, and Newton, and more contemporary scholars such as Einstein. Many theoretical problems have their genesis in day-to-day encounters and experiences of scientists and practitioners as well as philosophers. The importance of providing humans with augmented capability to solve problems and make decisions has created both theoretical and applied problems. Turing's (1950) work in automata theory provided the basis for the development of sophisticated data processing technologies, which in turn has directed the attention of psychologists, sociologists, and other scientists to practical problems in education, management, decision making, and problem solving.

With these thoughts in mind, our goal is to examine briefly the methods used by information professionals to collect data and evaluate hypotheses using models, simulations, exercises, and games.

CLASSIC METHODOLOGY

From the great thinkers like Aristotle and Plato comes a tradition of dealing with uncertainty. Emphasis is placed on logic or *deductive thinking*. An observation leads to a *proposition*, a declarative statement about the observation in question. Logic and observation enable one to state a number of axioms, propositions that are accepted as true without requiring proof. The inductive method, however, starts with observations from which a hypothesis (or guess) is generated. The hypothesis is tested through experimentation. Replication of the experiment is fundamental to the negation or affirmation of the hypothesis. In the inductive method, the data affirm or deny the hypothesis.

In classic methodology, as outlined in his famous statement regarding the testing of hypotheses, John Stuart Mill postulated the manner in which cause and effect could be established for particular observations or phenomena. Mill's concepts are foundations for the methodology used by scientists today. The procedure that is used to conduct the investigation or study is referred to as the *scientific method*. This method is *reductionistic* because it stresses the need to isolate and define specific variables relating to the phenomenon in question. The assumption is made that a particular phenomenon can be the result of (or influenced by) numerous factors. According to the scientific method, however, it is necessary to explore a *restricted* number of variables at a time and to study them under conditions that can be replicated by other investigators.

An important aspect of scientific method is the generation of a *hypothesis* about the phenomenon in question. A hypothesis is a statement that proposes some state or condition (factor) about a phenomenon we are interested in. The hypothesis should make clear the independent, dependent, and control variables. An example of the application of this method to an area of interest to information scientists will illustrate these concepts.

One question that has intrigued psychologists, educators, parents, and information scientists concerns the age at which computers should be introduced to the child (Beeson and Williams 1986). Presumably there may be some benefit to introducing computers early in life. To what extent do preschool children select interaction with computers from among other activities available to them? Do age and gender influence choice? These questions can be framed in the form of a hypothesis that proposes that gender and age are important variables in a child's choice of activity-- particularly computers. Gender and age are the independent variables and the choice of activity the dependent (resultant) variable. Beeson and Williams studied age by establishing two groups (under 5 years of age and over 5 years of age). The dependent variable represented the child's selection among many different options, such as blocks, wheeled vehicles, a playhouse, and the computer. If the investigators suspected that family economic status would be an important independent variable, but did not want to determine the effects, they would keep this variable constant; the

45

children would come from families representing a specific economic class.   Economic class would be under the *control* of the investigation. This is what is meant by *control variable*. Incidentally, the investigators found no difference between male and female preschool children in selecting computer activity, nor did preschool age make a difference in the choice of computers as a preferred activity option.

Data Collection

Because of the nature of the problems that information professionals face, methods for collecting data are important to the information literature.   The methods we discuss are surveys, questionnaires, opinion polls, brainstorming, and case histories.

Surveys, Questionnaires, Interviews, and Polls

These four methods are grouped together because, more often than not, surveys use the techniques of questionnaires, interviews, and polling. Surveys, using questionnaires, interviews, and polls, have been applied to a number of problems of interest to information professionals. For example, they have been conducted to study the use of periodicals (e.g., journals) and other materials in the library (e.g., monographs, reports); the increase in number of publications; the habits of users in seeking information; and the different patterns of information use by corporate executives. In these studies, the most popular instrument is the questionnaire: a list of items that probe the respondents' attitudes or practices regarding matters (variables) that the investigator deems important to the area of interest.

Polls, on the other hand, are directed more at opinions and beliefs. They are quite popular during political events, when they are used to determine the probability of a given outcome. Quite often polling is done on a one-on-one basis, that is, an inquiry over the telephone, a letter sent to many individuals, or a home or office visit by the pollster. The assumption is made that the polling of individuals when aggregated will reflect the opinions and attitudes of the group or part of a population.

Interviews and questionnaires are powerful research tools. Data on individual experience and behavior can sometimes only be obtained in this way. Perceptions, attitude, and opinions cannot be easily inferred through observation but are accessible through interviews. It is basic to the success of the outcome of interviewing that the interviewer explain what the research is trying to achieve, how the respondent was chosen, who is conducting this research, and that the respondent will remain anonymous. Equally important is that the questions be carefully worded and posed in an identical fashion to all interviewees. Some probing may be undertaken but only to help stimulate a response. The questions must not be altered. Finally, the response must be recorded, preferably during the interview. The interviewer may use several kinds of recording devices, including taking extensive notes.

Sampling

In all methods included under the heading of surveys, a very critical problem is *sampling*. Sampling simply means determining the characteristics of the population that one wishes to study or investigate. It includes the number of individuals to be studied, in addition to their characteristics, so as to render the results reliable and valid. The problems of sampling are reflected in the following:

> ... it is not sufficient to ensure that the sampling frame includes a representative sample of users. It is also necessary to ensure that states of research, types of data, types of information usage, channels of communication, and types of user behaviour are adequately represented in the sampling frame. (Menzel 1964)

In the 1981 University of Pittsburgh manpower study described in chapter 2, the sample population included respondents from industry, government, and academia. The distribution of respondents in each category was selected to provide results that would be representative of the population of individuals in that group.

Critical Discourse

Information professionals, like other professionals, use opinion and comment among themselves (individually or collectively) as part of their approaches to understanding events and experiences. Comment (or discourse) allows for active exchange of ideas while implicitly verifying the logic of these ideas for their defense. It provides clues as to the factors that may be important in the problem.

Generally, critical discourse is related to some standard upon which the event or experience can be judged. Political debates are an example of critical discourse. They provide a forum for the airing of ideas on policy and other issues that are argued against counter-ideas and positions. The standard in this case is considered part of the outcome; namely, that whatever arguments or ideas are posed, they should meet the criterion of face validity, that the positions taken were credible against the collective sense of reality.

Brainstorming

Brainstorming is a process in which new ideas and concepts emerge through mutual exchange. Implied in the process is that the outcome of the experience will provide insight to the problems or issues at hand. Unfortunately, little documentation is available in the literature on the use and effectiveness of this technique. Those who support brainstorming rest their case on the idea that when everything else fails in the resolution of the problem, a brainstorming session may help.

Case Histories

A case history is a detailed account of the processes and outcomes associated with a particular phenomenon. Many notable case histories have been produced in the physical sciences in the careful documentation that precedes new inventions and discoveries, as well as the generation of new theories. Japan, for example, used case histories to study medical problems resulting from the detonation of the atomic bomb. Documentation on the illnesses incurred by

American servicemen as the result of Agent Orange is another example. Case studies are excellent sources for the development of hypotheses, which can then be tested through experimentation.

Models, Simulations, and Exercises

Another way information professionals make decisions in complex situations is to approximate the situation and investigate outcomes for the idealized system. Building a model or developing a simulation is often much less expensive and risky than building an information system based on untested hypotheses.

Modeling

Modeling refers to the practice of generating a mathematical representation of reality. The following assumptions can be made about models:

All thinking is basically grounded on constructs and concepts of ideas as models.

Any mode of human thought that employs labels or causal theories is a form of modeling. (Meadows 1984)

A model is a form of analogy, a metaphor.

A model may be inductive or deductive.
Inductive: Predictive of findings on living systems that are not available from observation.
Deductive: Displays known relationships and characteristics of some living system or set of them. (Miller 1978)

A model is a conceptual (abstract) approximation of a concrete or real system. It cannot provide us with absolute answers to questions because it is an idealized representation of the thing we want to understand. It is often impossible to include in a model all the variables that represent a complex phenomenon in its entirety. For example, modeling a living system is next to impossible because of the innumerable variables that influence its existence. Even if we were able to identify these variables, the amount of data required to apply the model in a simulation would be prohibitive in terms of both time and cost.

> . . . as knowledge increases, the corresponding models grow more complex. The building of such highly complex models involves considerable expenditure of time and resources. But the use of such models in the decision-making process is justified only when the laws by which the phenomenon under investigation operate are well known, and when widely recognized and pragmatically tested mathematical descriptions are available. (Gelovani 1984)

Others have differentiated between *system models* and *process models*. A system model describes the structure of the model by means of interconnected components. Environmental engineers often build huge, vastly complex system models of river systems, for example, to study the effects of channelization or dams. A process model describes the changes that occur between the parts along the path of the system. Economic models that attempt to predict future oil prices based on numerous idealized inputs are examples of process models. Sometimes a particular model can include both structural components and process functions. In addition, a model can integrate several conceptual frameworks.

Mathematical expressions describing particular relationships among variables also serve as conceptual models. For instance, the relationship among the physical dimensions of a right triangle can be expressed by the well-known mathematical equation $c^2 = a^2 + b^2$. Mathematical expressions vary in complexity relative to the number of processes and structures they wish to describe.

Simulation

A simulation attempts to imitate some part of reality. Some claim that there is no distinction between simulation and modeling. Certain conclusions, however can be drawn from the literature that enable us to take the position that, although modeling and simulation are related, they perform different functions and different principles can be applied to them.

Simulations are based on models, mathematical abstractions of certain aspects of reality. These models could range from generalized conceptualizations to carefully quantified (mathematical) expressions of the reality in question. A model is a static set of abstractions to which isolated inputs are fed. A simulation is a model moved through space and time, being fed a continuous series of inputs. Simulations based on such models are seen as a means for testing the model, rather than as the model itself. Humans often build models that arise either through fancy or through concrete analysis. Prior to their first attempt at flying the object they envisioned, the Wright brothers at Cooke Field in Dayton, Ohio, conceptualized what an actual object could do, and only then did they build a physical version or prototype. Later, under actual field conditions, with a fabricated object they called a flying machine, they simulated flight conditions. It was only after many simulations and many changes to the initial model that they were able to execute a heavier-than-air flight successfully. A static model of the physical realities of flying a helicopter serves as the basis for an interactive flight simulator.

C. F. Hermann (1967) provided a compendium of criteria that we can use to evaluate simulations:

1. Repeatability of outcomes: The results from one execution of a simulation should correspond to outcomes from other executions of the simulations under the same conditions.

2. Face validity: Is the simulation credible? Are the inputs reasonable approximations of likely real world events? If we are trying to simulate an unlikely condition, face validity is reduced.

3. Variable validity: The conditions or processes from the real world that we are attempting to study should be as close as possible to those in real life. Inclusions or exclusions of ad hoc characteristics that depart from the reality of the situation will tend to decrease the validity of the simulation. This kind of validity may be difficult to achieve because real-life situations often represent a

complex combination of variables that are difficult to represent.

4. Event credibility: This refers to the similarity of the simulation to the real-life situation. The extent of similarity has to be agreed upon prior to actual implementation of the simulation.

5. Hypothesis validity: The simulation should be guided by an objective that is grounded on a hypothesis concerning the variables that are under study and for which the method of simulation is applied. In other words, the hypothesis should be specific as to the characteristics of the system. If the hypothesis guiding the simulation is not specific, the findings could be less valid because of inability of the simulation to show the relationship between the characteristics of the problem and the outcome.

These validity checks can be supplemented by other aspects of simulations that scientists have used as part of their investigatory work. For example, the method of analyzing data derived from simulations is particularly critical. As in experimentation, it is desirable that this be determined before the simulation is undertaken. There are several reasons for this recommendation.

First the *amount of data* required for one type of analysis may be too great in terms of time and money to support the benefits from the simulation. Second, simulations are particularly vulnerable to *variable confounding*: the practice of defining a variable in a number of ways and then selecting the definition that best suits the data obtained. Preanalysis on this issue can increase the validity of the simulation. Finally, *documentation* of the step-by-step flow of the system is critical to the validity of the simulation. With the use of computer simulations, this problem is lessened but should be kept in mind.

For simulations that study human interaction and individual performance in a system context, motivation is a highly volatile variable that must be accounted for. If one knows that a situation is real one tends to respond differently than if one knows the situation is fabricated. The psychological impact and the consequences of an action are different.

Exercising

Exercising was first used by scientists working at the MITRE Corporation System Design Laboratory, Lexington, Massachusetts, in 1961. Exercising, as a method for analysis, was an outcome from simulations that were conducted at the time to determine military officer behavior in command-control-communication (C^3) environments. As discussed previously, it was reasoned if the personnel in question knew that an activity was a simulation, their performance would be influenced by that factor. To counter this motivational variable, the orientation was changed from a simulation to an exercise. Exercising attempts to negate the psychological effects on performance associated with simulations by monitoring the performance of participants both individually and cumulatively and requiring that they excel relative to predetermined criteria. Nuclear power plants often conduct "simulations" to determine the response of individuals to certain contingencies that could occur in that environment. Such simulations are actually exercises to the extent that the optimum system flows have been predetermined, response rules established for certain contingencies (from previous simulations, either conceptual or mathematical), and their purpose is to arrive at a point of readiness in case of unforeseen emergencies (plant failures). Public school fire drills are a familiar example of an exercise. In essence, such experiences often fall under the rubric of training, a term synonymous with other terms of exercising.

Gaming

Gaming is a form of simulation in which opposing elements of a conflict are represented. Generally, a game is based on a model in which the variables represent relevant environmental events and functions.

Many simulations of real-life situations where individuals have to make decisions are referred to as games. The scenarios usually are generated by computers, with individuals interacting among themselves, as well as with the computer. A political/military exercise (PME) falls in this pattern (developed by Rand Corporation in 1954). The PME is a kind of war game where the participants are professionals (political or military) and where the structure permits a test of foreign policy options with feedback in the form of simulations of the impact or consequences of the decisions. In the United States, a scenario of this kind took place on television (*An Exercise in Defense Management*, CBS, 1984). Actual political figures, in conjunction with military officers, were asked to respond to certain hypothetical situations in which adversary problems could be initiated and resolutions proposed.

Game theory, which is the basis of gaming, is defined as "mathematical logic applied to determine the various possibilities of maximizing gain or minimizing loss in games or in business situations; the choice of strategy is dictated by the likeliest mathematical possibility" (Mandel 1977). Based on mathematical formulations, the theory attempts to develop quantitative means for understanding the interactions among individuals and groups under specific kinds of scripted situations. The concept of game theory can be applied to economics, and specifically to utility, the worth of a particular option and its outcome to the individual or group. Mathematical equations are established that represent a model of the situational variable in question.

Statistical Methods

Once data are collected, the information professional must determine their significance. Numerous statistical methods can be applied to data evaluation. It is beyond the scope of this book to provide a detailed account of these techniques, or for that matter to inventory all the approaches that are available. The reader should refer to the literature on statistical method for information on evaluative techniques such as indicators of central tendency and variability, linear models, relationship and correlation, regression analysis, content analysis, and sociometry.

INTERDISCIPLINARITY AS A PROBLEM-SOLVING METHOD

Interdisciplinarity can be considered to be a method of bringing together several disciplines and synthesizing their contributions to a specific problem, which is necessary for collaboration in information science. Interdisciplinary thinking addressed the fact that problems cannot be pigeonholed according to academic disciplines but, rather, that a great deal of overlap exists among areas of study that are represented in an information science problem. Each discipline needs the findings generated by others as a check on the validity of its own generalizations and theories. Validity in this context means the ability of theoretical formulations to make accurate predictions and eventually to be translated into means for control of the phenomena in question. Thus, the best way currently available to check the validity of generalization and theories in the science is to evaluate them against the findings gathered on equivalent or related problems by scientific disciplines. This evaluation must occur, however, before the application is attempted.

The problem for information science is to determine what it must take from other disciplines in terms of perspectives in solving a problem. It is through this means that information science can begin to understand the ways it should collaborate with these other fields in developing its own theoretical structure. Interchange eventually lends insight into the variables that must be included in research design as well as providing a basis for generating hypotheses that are testable and productive.

REFERENCES

Beeson, Betty Spillers, and R. Ann Williams. "The Effect of Gender and Age on Preschool Children's Choice of the Computer as a Child-Selected Activity." *JASIS* 36 (1985):339-44.

Brittain, J. M. "Information Needs and Application of the Results of User Studies." In *Perspectives in Information Science*, edited by A. Debons and W. Cameron. Leyden: Noordhoff, 1975, 431.

Festinger, Leon, and David Katz, eds. *Research Methods in the Behavioral Sciences*. New York: Holt, Rinehart, Winston, 1953, 331, 354-58.

Gelovani, Viktor A. "An Interactive Modeling System as a Tool for Analyzing Complex Socio-Economic Problems." In *Models of Reality*, edited by Jacques Richardson. Mt. Airy, Md.: Lomond Books, 1984, 79.

Hermann, C. F. "Validation Problems in Games and Simulations with Special Reference to Models of International Politics." *Behavior Science* 12 (1967):219.

Lewin, Kurt. "Formalization and Progress in Psychology." In *Field Theory in Social Science: Selected Theoretical Papers*, edited by D. Cartwright. New York: Harper, 1951.

Mandel, Siegfried. *Dictionary of Science*. New York: Dell, 1977, 149, 303.

Meadows, Dennis. "On Modeling, Limits and Understanding." In *Models of Reality*, edited by Jacques Richardson. Mt. Airy, Md.: Hammond Books, 1984.

Manzel, H. "The Information Needs of Current Scientific Research." *Library Quarterly* 34, no. 1 (1964):4-19.

Miller, J. G., ed. *Living Systems*. New York: McGraw-Hill, 1978.

Richardson, Jacques, ed. "A Primer of Model Systems." In *Models of Reality*, edited by Jacques Richardson. Mt. Airy, Md.: Hammond Books, 1984.

Turing, Alan M. "Computing Machinery and Intelligence." *Mind* 59 (October 1950):433-60.

4
Systems Theory and Information Science

In daily life we refer to systems quite freely. There are transportation systems, health care systems, financial systems, and so on. A good definition is provided by Hall and Fagan (de Greene 1970): "A system is a set of objects together with the relationships between the objects and between their attributes." Ackoff and Emery (1972) described a system as "a set of interrelated elements, each of which is related directly or indirectly to every other element, and no subset of which is unrelated to any other subset."

There are two approaches to understanding systems: to examine the most influential theories and to look at the kinds of systems that exist and are discussed in the literature.

SYSTEMS THEORIES

One of the most important theories about what a system is and how it works is general systems theory. It attempts to uncover some general principles related to systems in the broadest sense, and then to identify the role of the various disciplines that contribute to this understanding. Kenneth E. Boulding (1968), who first proposed General Systems Theory, wrote, "The objectives of general systems theory then can be set out with varying degrees of ambition and confidence. At a low level of ambition but with a high degree of confidence it aims to point out similarities in the theoretical constructions of different disciplines, where these exist, and to develop theoretical models having applicability to at least two different fields of study. At a higher level of ambition, but with perhaps a lower degree of confidence it hopes to develop something like a spectrum of theories--a system of systems which may perform the function of a gestalt in theoretical construction. Such gestalts in special fields have been of great value in directing research towards the gaps which they reveal."

Bertalanffy (1968), another prominent general systems theorist, repeated these assertions stated above with minor variation: "General systems theory . . . [means] to derive from a general definition of 'system' a complex of interacting components, concepts characteristic of organized wholes such as interaction, sum, mechanization, centralization, competition, finality, etc., and to apply them to concrete phenomena."

K. M. Khailov (1968) applied the concept of general systems theory to biological entities, stating, "The theory unites the fundamental principles of organization and encompasses most diverse natural, social, and intellectual phenomena."

> The general living systems theory . . . is a conceptual system concerned primarily with concrete systems which exist in space and time. . . . These systems . . . can be identified at seven hierarchical levels . . ., cell, organ, organism, group, organization, society, and supranational system . . . All these levels are open systems composed of subsystems which process inputs, throughputs, and outputs of various forms of matter, energy, and information. A concrete, real, or veridical system is a non-random accumulation of matter and energy in a region in physical space-time, which is organized into interacting, interrelated subsystems or components. (Miller 1987)

In understanding general systems theory and perhaps systems theory in the broadest sense, it is necessary to understand what is meant by the *systems approach*. The systems approach is a way of looking at the world from the point of view of interacting elements, each directly influencing the others. Churchman (1971) related this concept to weltanschauung, or world view. Thus, general systems theory is the embodiment of the systems approach, translating the influences of each part to the whole in an interactive chain, and determining those principles that describe and define these interactions.

Another important concept about systems in general and how they work is systems theory. This deals with specific systems and the principles governing their structure and function. It is concerned with *categorizing* concrete models of systems, that is, with identifying types of systems. There are various views as to the nature of systems theory. The following views emerge from an analysis by Machlup and Mansfield (1983).

1. There is no general agreement as to the scope of systems theory.

2. Systems theory is primarily mathematical.

3. Systems theory is not a theory of concrete systems but a theory of models. It does not accept responsibility for the accuracy or relevance of these models.

4. Systems theory contributes to the other sciences by generating a set of models for any well-defined system, but does not specify which model is best for a particular system.

5. Systems theory is reductionistic. Reductionism refers to attempts to isolate specific variables that influence a phenomenon for study.

6. Systems theory can provide the basis for organizing the social sciences.

7. While general systems theory deals with the most fundamental, abstract, and general aspects of systems, systems theory deals with more specific questions about more well-defined kinds of systems.

The more specific nature of systems theory changes the way its adherents define what a system is. The ideas of objective, purpose, and goal were of central interest to Ackoff and Emery in delineating the boundaries of discrete individual systems and categorizing them according to type. Their treatment of the issue (1972) differentiates between two basic kinds of systems:

Abstract Systems

An abstract system is one in which all the elements that make up the system are *concepts*. Concepts are articulated sets of functional properties and relationships. Written and spoken languages are abstract systems, as is our mathematical system. Words and numerals are conceptual in nature; they exist only in the abstract.

Concrete Systems

A concrete system is a system in which at least two elements are tangible objects. Concrete systems are specific entities that exist in space and time. They relate to nonrandom accumulations of nature and energy in a region of physical space and time. These energies are organized into interactive, interrelated subsystems or components (e.g., cells, groups, or organizations). The exact boundaries of a concrete system, however, may be a matter of opinion. A human being is a concrete system. The system of numerals and letters by which we represent abstract mathematical and linguistic concepts is also a concrete system.

The literature provides several useful categories to describe different types of concrete systems. Some of the most important and interesting of these are listed below.

Purposeful Systems

A purposeful system can change its goals in a constant or changing environment (McCormick and Sanders 1982). Alternatively, Ackoff and Emery (1972) define a purposeful system as one that can pursue the same goal across changing conditions by adapting its behavior. Living systems are purposeful systems; they adapt to survive.

Closed Systems

A closed system is a concrete system whose boundaries are impermeable to the transmission of matter, energy, or data, both into the system from the environment and from the environment into the system. The system can be completely closed; it is useful, however, to refer to the degree to which a system may be closed. The biosphere of earth, for example, is a closed system to the extent that its atmosphere serves as a boundary, absorbing or reflecting matter and energy.

Open Systems

An open system is a concrete system whose boundaries are open or permeable by matter, energy, and data. As with closed systems, it is reasonable only to refer to the degree to which a given system is open. Any living system is open to the extent that it takes in matter (as by eating) and energy (as through the senses), and in return creates sounds, gives off heat, eliminates wastes, and so forth.

Action Structures

Ackoff and Emery proposed another way to categorize systems in terms of the likely actions they take and the outcomes of these actions relative to the environment in which they operate (fig. 4.1).

FUNCTIONS OF OUTCOMES

	A. UNI-UNI One function in all environments	B. UNI-MILTI One function in any one environment, different functions in some different environments	C. MULTI-MULTI Different functions in same and different environments
1. UNI-UNI One structure in all environments	1A. PASSIVE FUNCTIONAL (meters)	1B. PASSIVE MULTIFUNCTIONAL (waste emitters)	
2. UNI-MULTI One structure in any one environment, different structures in some different environments	2A. REACTIVE FUNCTIONAL (servomechanisms)	2B. REACTIVE MULTIFUNCTIONAL (industrial robots)	
3. MULTI-MULTI Different structures in same and different environments	3A. ACTIVE FUNCTIONAL GOAL-SEEKING (single-program automata)	3B. ACTIVE MULTIFUNCTIONAL MULTI-GOAL-SEEKING (multiprogram automata)	3C. ACTIVE MULTIFUNCTIONAL AND ENVIRONMENTALLY INDEPENDENT PURPOSEFUL (people)

STRUCTURE OF ACTIONS

Figure 4.1. Classes of Functional Individuals and Systems. (From Ackoff and Emery 1972. Reprinted with permission.)

To illustrate this point, consider the UNI-UNI action structure, which refers to a unit of measurement or action. A ruler or measuring tape is a good example. Measuring the width of a room with a ruler or measuring tape provides us with a way to deal with our environment, but these tools can be used in other physical space-time environments as well. Ackoff and Emery called such items "passive functional." A water bucket is another structure that can be applied in several environments (passive multifunctional); however, it can be applied differently in different environments (UNI-MULTI). It can be used to carry any number of items and also used to cover things.

Churchman's System Model

Another perspective on systems is provided by C. W. Churchman, a philosopher and professor of business administration at the University of California, Berkeley. He loosely defined a system as "a structure that has organized components." In his view, the characteristics of a system are as follows:

1.   It is teleological (purposeful).

2.   You can determine its performance.

3.   It has a user or users.

4.   It has parts (components) that in and of themselves have purpose.

5.   It is embedded in an environment.

6.   It includes a decision maker who is internal to the system and who can change the performance of the parts.

7.   There is a designer who is concerned with the structure of the system and whose conceptualization of the system can direct the actions of the decision maker and ultimately affect the end result of the actions of the entire system.

8.   The designer's purpose is to change a system so as to maximize its value to the user.

9.   The designer ensures that the system is stable to the extent that he or she knows its structure and function.

Churchman's concept regarding information is relevant to information science in general and information systems in particular. In his view, information systems allow us to gain knowledge. Although he did not explicitly make a distinction between information and knowledge as we have done, his writing implies such a distinction: "Knowledge can be considered as a collection of information, or as an action, or as a potential" (Churchman 1971).

The matter of gaining knowledge centers around the process of inquiry--looking into, probing, asking questions.   Churchman detailed several systems of inquiry from the history of philosophical thinking that differentiate the methods for inquiry.   These are summarized in table 4.1. From this table, one can surmise that each system of inquiry has as its basis a characteristic world view.

For the design of information systems, the important conclusion to be drawn from Churchman's analysis of inquiry systems is that the way we perceive and conceptualize events influences the way we structure information systems that enable us to deal with events. The way we view the world influences the way we design information systems (e.g., structuring the system with an emphasis on technology rather than on the user) and ultimately in the way we orient ourselves to ask questions and invoke the information system to augment our human capabilities.

Table 4.1

Summary of Churchman's Inquiry Systems

Philosopher	*World View*
Leibnitz	Everyone has innate ideas. Everyone begins with the same mental "baseline." Everyone should produce the same solution to a problem.
Locke	Everyone starts with a blank mind. From observations one collects data. A single solution is produced through consensus.
Kant	Everyone begins with some a priori ideas. Data collection is colored by those ideas. At least two solutions are produced.

Hegel   Everyone begins with a common data base.
                          Data are observed by two totally different
                              world views.
                          Two contrary solutions are produced.

Singer   Everyone begins with a common data base.
                          If all observers agree, we are not looking
                              critically enough at the data.
                          Many solutions are produced.

Churchman's assertion that the structure of an information system is influenced by the designer's world view not only explains the vast spectrum of available information systems models, but demands that we now focus on specific information scientists and their views.

Generalized Information Systems Models

Models of information systems that fall in this category suggest that the components identified are germane to the system--they are both necessary and sufficient to the system's existence. In a sense, these models are *descriptive* rather than *explanatory*. They are not seen as representing a theory of information systems, but are perceptions of such systems that guide their study, analysis, and design.

Miller (1978) and Debons and Cameron (1975) attempted to provide an inclusive statement as to the structure of an information system. Two characteristics identify such models: (1) they represent an attempt to use the living organism as a basic conceptual structure (metaphor) for the information system. The basic tenets of this concept are physiological, that is, they pertain to the nature of body or organismic function; and (2) the components of an information system serve to establish and maintain intersystem and intrasystem stability (negentropy through feedback). To this extent information systems are cybernetic systems.

Miller's Living System Model

Miller provided an inclusive model of an information system within the biological framework of a *living system*. This approach considers the living system as capable of doing two things: processing matter and energy, and processing information. (What Miller refers to as information is data by our definition.) Living systems are open and concrete (as explained in our previous discussion), and hierarchical in character. Beyond their hierarchical character, Miller specified the two basic subsystems that are common to all living systems.

1. Subsystems that process matter and energy

Ingestor: Takes matter and energy from the environment.

Distributor: Distributes input to the other components of the system.

Converter: Changes the energy from one input to another to meet the needs of the components.

Producer: Lends stability to the system by establishing limits among the inputs (matter and energy), thereby ensuring that the system will survive.

Storage: Retains, for some time, what the system receives in the form of matter and energy.

Extruder: Emits from the system that which it produces as well as the wastes that are developed as the result of systemic processes.

Motor: Makes possible required action; this includes the action generated among the other components.

Supporter: Equalizes the components of the system so that each can function effectively.

2. Subsystems that process information

Input transducer: The sensory subsystem that brings symbols into the system, changing them to other forms to transmit to the components of the system as data.

Internal transducer: The sensory subsystem that receives data from other components and subsystems and changes their form to make them suitable for retransmission within the system.

Channel and net: Route matter and energy in the system (interconnected components and parts).

Decoder: Processes the signal (data) it receives from the internal transducer from one form to another so that it can be used by the system.

Associator: Ties one form of data to another, thereby creating significant relationships. (Miller referred to this as the first stage of the learning process; he called data "markers bearing information.")

Memory: Stores data that are established at various times.

Decider: Regulates the flow of data among various parts of the system, thereby controlling the entire system.

Encoder: Takes data obtained from the components of the system and attempts to make it understandable to other systems in its environment.

Output transducer: "Puts out markers bearing information . . ." and changes "markers within the system into other matter-energy forms" to be transmitted over the system's channels. (Although Miller did not refer to this as a data display, this is the essence of what he meant.)

Debons's EATPUT Model

Another generalized information system model is suggested by Debons (1961; fig. 4.2). Its fundamental structure consists of six basic components, the first letters of which, taken together as an acronym, spell EATPUT.

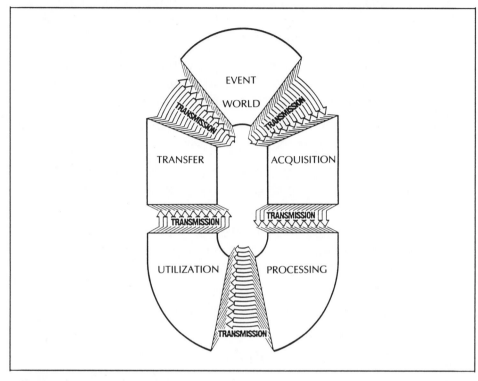

Figure 4.2. Debons's Information System Model. (From Morton 1985. Reprinted with permission.)

Debons claims these components generalize the basic structure of all information systems, both organismic technological. The six components are as follows:

1. Event world: The occurrences that are relevant to the objective and functioning of the information system. It includes the process of classifying and categorizing events, and the linguistic representation of them in the form of symbols.

2. Acquisition: The initial physical component of the system, used to capture matter and energy (the event) from the external environment.

3. Transmission: The actual movement of signals (data) within and between the components of the system.

4. Processing: The ordering, storage, and retrieval of data for the ultimate purpose of applying it to problem solving, decision making, or general development (knowledge formulation).

5. Utilization: The component that represents the evaluative, interpretive requirement of information systems, similar to Miller's decider function.

6. Transfer: The action component of the system; the implementation of the decider function through the system's transfer medium. The transfer function in this model can be seen as communication or information transfer, two terms that are at times used similarly in the literature.

The EATPUT model describes an information system as a nonlinear, recursive system. Each component acts within as well as outside of itself. This means that each component of the system contains its own EATPUT substructure, with acquisition, transmission, and so on occurring internally, in addition to the component's wider function. Both Miller's information processing model and Debons's EATPUT model view living systems as information systems. In his description of the EATPUT model, Debons claimed that when technology is coupled with a corresponding organic counterpart (e.g., radar and the eye), a man-machine system emerges, the objective of which is to augment human functioning. Thus, the model represents an attempt to provide guidelines for the analysis and design of information systems whereby human limitations are compensated for by technological capabilities that extend human functioning.

An important point to stress in our understanding of these two perceptions of information systems is that they are similar in componential structure (sensing, processing, action) to what is referred to in the literature as *human information processing systems* (fig. 4.3). The human processing model indicated in figure 4.3 is used by behavioral scientists in their attempt to depict the process involved in the human brain (cognitive system) in dealing with input data, while the Miller and Debons models attempt to provide a more generalized concept of the information system of which the human brain is part.

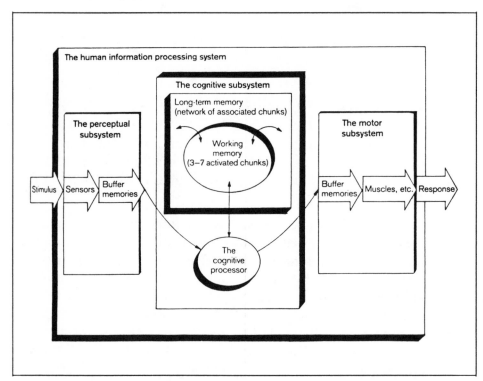

Figure 4.3. An Overview of the Human Information Processing System. (From Harmon and King 1985. Reprinted with permission.)

Component-oriented Information Systems Models

In addition to the models presented by Miller and Debons, several other models represent statements on the nature and function of components (subsystems) of information systems. They are hypothetical statements about certain specific aspects or parts of information systems, and describe the nature and function of components of such systems rather than dealing with the whole information system as we define it.

Yovits's Model

Marshall Yovits (Whittemore and Yovits 1974), physicist, computer scientist, and information scientist, presented a model of an information system based on the definitional assumption that information is data of value in decision making. The scope of Yovits's is analogous to that of the utilization component of the EATPUT model (fig. 4.4). The critical assumption underlying Yovits's model is that the information system provides data in response to the action that the user takes in responding to events. In other words, the data received from the action taken provide feedback (information) to the user. Because of this information (data of value), the user *learns* to deal with events. A similar expression of this theory proposes that the consummation of a decision leads to information (Barnes 1975).

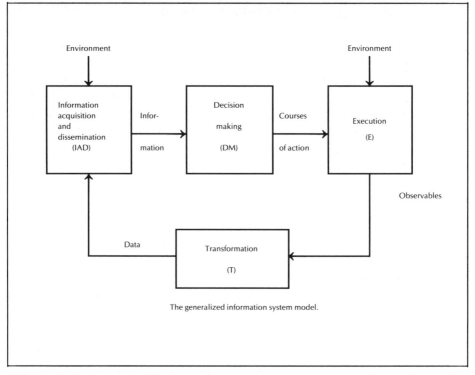

Figure 4.4. Yovits's Model. (From Whittemore and Yovits 1973. Reprinted with permission.)

Samuelson's Model

Another model of an information system that focuses on decision making, and hence on the utilization component, is that of Kjell Samuelson (1973). Samuelson is a physician as well as an information scientist, and his model reflects this perspective.

Samuelson attempted to detail the cognitive process involved in diagnosing patients' illnesses. He differentiated two basic segments of such systems: the information field, which provides the data for action, and the object field, which includes action taken after that are obtained.

It should be noted that Samuelson actually endorsed the Yovits hypothesis, as the ultimate objective of the system is diagnosis, and that the data gained from the diagnosis enable the generation of information to support them.

Shannon's Model

Claude Shannon's theory of information is incorporated in a model of a *communication system* (fig. 4.5). This model is another case of detailing one component of an information system, namely, *transfer*.

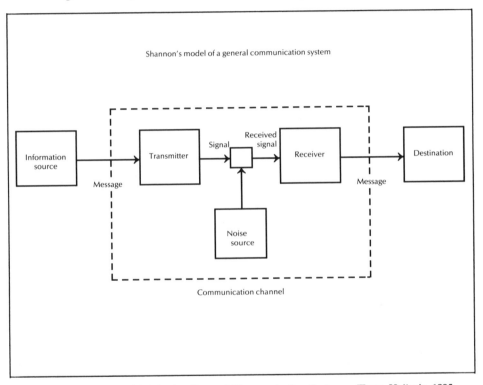

Figure 4.5. Shannon's Model of a General Communication System. (From Heilprin 1985. Reprinted with permission.)

Although many professionals consider this model to describe an information system, it actually is a statement on the transmission of signals in a physical transporter (channel). Nevertheless, the importance of Shannon's concept of information lies in its attempt to be quantitative in dealing with a phenomenon that is ambiguously defined and often misrepresented.

Shannon's formula for information is represented by mathematical expressions based on the possibility of certain alternative states of an event and the likely change in state of the receiver. There are basically two formulas: one assumes the equal likelihood of occurrences or states; the other assumes unequal likelihood of occurrences or states.

Heilprin's Model ✳

Laurence Heilprin, physicist and information scientist, related the concept of information to a cybernetic framework, thus combining Shannon's concept of information with principles of human cognition and communication. He stated "An abstract, skeletal but comprehensive view of information science may be had by considering the flow of information between the information recipient and the environment" (1985).

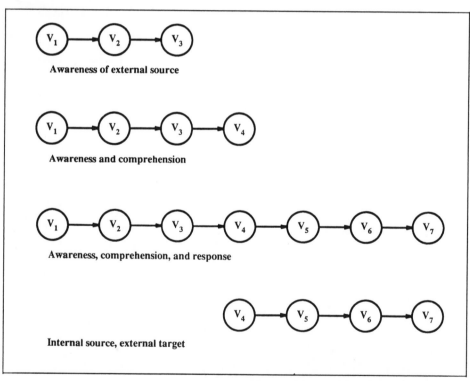

Figure 4.6. Heilprin's Vector System. (From Heilprin 1985. Reprinted with permission.)

The aim of Heilprin's model is mathematically to specify the vectors (processes or forces) that influence the interaction among the constituents of the sender and receiver.

Heilprin identified vectors at several levels, as shown in figures 4.6 and 4.7. Figure 4.6 shows that forces (vectors) are emitted from external sources (event world) creating a state of awareness (information) in the internal source. These forces extend awareness to a state of comprehension (knowledge) represented by forces that are part of the cognitive function (V^4, V^5, V^6, V^7), which ultimately lead to action (on an external target) by the original sender. This is an attempt by Heilprin to relate the communicative process (indicated in figure 4.6) to the internal processes that precede and are a part of it. In figure 4.7 Heilprin sketches the same vector systems in a conceptualized communication or transfer system.

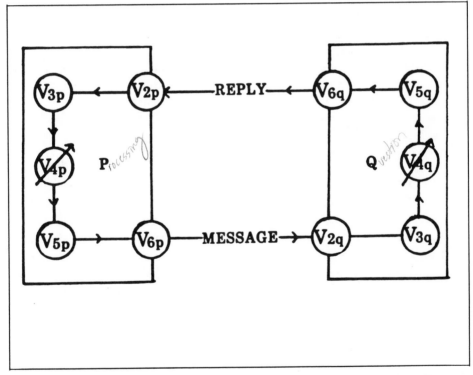

Figure 4.7. Two-way One-one Communication, V_{4p} to V_{4q} with Arbitrary Reply. (From Heilprin 1985. Reprinted with permission.)

Otten's Model

Klaus Otten, an electronics engineer and information scientist, provides another version of the communication (transfer) model. Again the formulations are *component-specific*, that is, an attempt to describe and quantify the factors that are central to transfer or implementation of action after action is formulated. Otten's conceptualization of the relationship between information and communication is best explained in his own words.

> "Information," conceived as state changes within an information system, is manifested at various levels within the system's interpretation processing hierarchy and serves various specific functions. According to the level of concern one can therefore distinguish between physical (carrier signal level), syntactic (code word level), semantic (isolated action trigger levels), and pragmatic (systems behavioral level) information. Accordingly, any reference to "information" should be specific and relative to the level at which the state changes serve a systems function. This qualifying statement appears necessary in addition to that which identifies the system (because information is inherently system-specific) and that which identifies the environmental relationship (the environment as perceivable and actually perceived by the system). (Otten 1975)

Because Otten saw information as directly related to or synonymous with communication, that is, the transmission of signals as well as the transporting or conveying of meaning, his theory delineates four levels of transfer. The first transfer level is the transfer of the energy contained in the event to *signals* that the transmission media can propagate. At the second level, the signals are combined to form *codes*. At the third level, codes are interpreted by the receiver. At the fourth and final level, action is taken based on what has been received.

The models that have been briefly discussed are but a small sample of those that can be classified as being related directly or indirectly to information systems or to one or more components of them. It is important to keep in mind that the distinction between general information system and component-specific models is blurred in the information science literature.

Another distinction further compounds the blurred conceptualization of what constitutes an information system. There is a class of information system models that are designated by function, such as management information systems, decision support systems, expert systems, and so on. To complete our overview of information system models, we must take a look at some of these.

Function-oriented Systems

Function-oriented systems are most often component-oriented systems although they stress particular activities, such as management, document retrieval, diagnosis, and so on. By and large, function-oriented systems, because of their heavy emphasis on data processing to achieve the functions desired, are more directly the province of computer science. Because of their importance to the interests of information scientists, and their interdisciplinary requirements, management, diagnostic, and service-oriented models deserve our attention.

Management Information Systems

Perhaps the most well-publicized of function-oriented information systems are management information systems (MIS). These systems combine aspects of management theory with aspects of data processing and communication theory.

There are numerous versions of management information systems, and the concepts underlying them can be easily understood. For an organization to survive, it must be able to plan, operate, direct, and control its resources. This can be considered to be the classic definition of management. Planning, operating, directing, and controlling persons and machinery are directed toward some objective, generally, producing or manufacturing goods and supplies, providing services, and other enterprises associated with commerce. As part of these objectives, numerous transactions are entailed, such as purchasing, disbursing, and so on (operational departments). Management information systems help automate routine management decisions by providing computer models that process specific data inputs and provide data for basic decisions. A good modern MIS often provides software support for figuring out opportunity costs over time, doing simple bookkeeping, updating inventory, and making other routine decisions that managers (most often middle managers) face.

Information Management Systems

Confusion often exists between management information systems and information management systems. Whereas management information systems provide the basis for aiding managers in planning and controlling an organization, information management systems (IMS) do exactly what their title suggests--they help manage information, better referred to as data in this context. They provide the basis for the management of information resources that exist in an organization. These resources include the acquisition of data and documents, the corporate library or information center, the accounting or comptroller's office, and the computer center and its associated data processing and user-oriented subunits.

Decision-Support Systems

Rapidly growing in importance, decision-support systems (DSS) provide support for the processing or decision-making components of the larger systems in which they are embedded.

The DSS started under the rubric of management decision systems. The concept initially referred to the role of interactive computer-based systems that could support unstructured decision making. It was slow to develop, although information scientists and others stressed the need for cooperation between humans and computers in decision making as early as 1960, when such a partnership was given the name man-computer symbiosis (Licklider 1960).

A DSS is in many ways similar to an MIS or any other information system, but the implications are different. An MIS is geared toward helping users solve structured problems, which come up from day to day and are predictable in terms of the steps required to solve them.

The DSS, on the other hand, is geared toward helping solve more unstructured types of problems: one-time challenges that require intuition, foresight, and brainstorming. It supports this kind of work with interactive graphics, database searching, program development tools, and so forth. The DSS is oriented toward supporting creative (as opposed to routine) problem solving, and is most cost-effective when applied to high-level management. The mechanisms are directed not as much to data processing but rather to the specific structuring of data presentation to aid decision-making and problem-solving functions. The general characteristics of a DSS as constructed by Scott (1986) are as follows.

1. It focuses on decision processes rather than transactions processing.

2. It is easily designed, simple in structure, and quickly implemented and altered.

3. It is designed and run by managers. *experts*

4. It provides information that is useful in a subsequent managerial analysis, rather than providing "the answer" or making a decision.

5. It is concerned with only one relatively small area of analysis or a small part of a large problem; more than one decision-support system may be used for a large problem or task.

6. It has logic that attempts to mimic the way a manager would analyze the same situation.

7. It has a data base that contains information extracted from other files of the organization and information from the external environment.

Evaluation stage

8. It permits the manager to test the probable results of alternative decisions, enabling the manager to answer such questions as, "What would be the effect on total sales and profits if I changed the sales discount?"

Expert Systems

Expert systems are aids to decision making and problem solving. They incorporate many of the characteristics of decision-support systems, but add another dimension, that of *artificial intelligence* (AI). As such, they represent the fusion of the data processing and utilization or interpretative components of information systems. They are actually knowledge systems, to the extent that they go beyond the cognitive level of awareness necessary for the acquisition of data. The following quotation discusses the relationship between AI and expert systems:

> The area of Artificial Intelligence (AI) has concentrated on the construction of higher performance programs in specialized professional domains, a pursuit that has encouraged an emphasis on the knowledge that underlies human expertise and has simultaneously decreased the apparent significance of domain-independent problem solving theory. . . . The area of expert systems investigates methods and techniques for constructing man-machine systems with specialized problem solving expertise. Expertise consists of knowledge about a particular domain, understanding of domain problems and skill in solving some of these problems. (Hayes-Roth, Waterman, and Lenat 1983)

Expert systems attempt to provide solutions by going through many of the same kinds of processes that a human expert unconsciously performs. Some systems are even built through careful, continuing study of a single expert. As shown in figure 4.8, expert systems consist of a few fundamental parts.

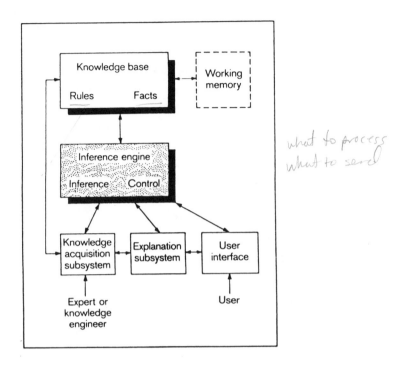

Figure 4.8. The Architecture of a Knowledge-Based Expert System. (The inference engine is shaded for emphasis.) (From Harmon and King 1985. Reprinted with permission.)

The fundamental idea is that reasoning is often done through manipulation of symbols. Reasoning is in this sense representational, or symbolic. As Newell (1980) indicated, the expert system includes "a broad class of systems capable of having and manipulating symbols."

The problems to which an expert system is applied must be sufficiently complicated to require an expert. Its focus is usually a very specific, narrow domain. The system must, within this domain, set up a mathematically describable progression of steps that it must go through to solve a problem. It must follow a set of rules about the problem, and, of course, questions must be asked of it in precisely the right way. The rules under which it operates enable the system to draw inferences, make judgments, and thereby solve complex problems that would otherwise require the application of human intelligence. Remember, however, that any intelligence the machine has *is* human intelligence, and that an expert system is program-driven like any other computer-based system. The components of an expert system are as follows:

1. Knowledge base: Includes the data gathered from individuals who can be referred to as experts. Stored in the knowledge base are not only the data that experts provide but logical relationships among the data elements.

2. Knowledge base management systems: Software that manages the stored facts (data) and experiences obtained from the experts when specific inferences demanded of the problem at hand are required.

3. Inference system: The logic in the combining of data from the experts so as to render insights (or solutions) to problems or decision (diagnostic) requirements.

Information Systems as Service Entities

Some view information systems as consisting of persons, technology, and related procedures that aid those who need information and/or knowledge as part of their work or profession, or for just the business of living. At times it is not clear whether the authors of these concepts consider the system to be the body of information, the container that includes this body of information, or that certain something that enables one to obtain the container of information and knowledge. We can assume that all of these inferences are possible. It is important to recognize, however, that different processes may be involved in dealing with the differences that are implied.

Havelock's Model

Havelock, a social psychologist interested in the use of knowledge among scientists, examined the ways in which scientists and other professionals obtain scientific and technical information and knowledge as part of their work. He considered information a physiological need, and as such, proposed a model of an environment, in the form of a clinic, that could meet this need. Havelock's description of such a clinic includes the related institutions (librarians, information centers, etc.) and procedures (links) that tie the constituent points together in a comprehensive knowledge-utilization social system.

Taylor's Model

Robert S. Taylor, of Syracuse University, referred to information systems in the plural as those environments of people, technologies, and procedures that include the following characteristics (1986):

1. They are formally designed processes that select, acquire, organize, store, retrieve, display, analyze, and/or interpret messages.

2. They are processes whereby messages are enhanced either by signals or by fundamental alteration of content.

3. Messages are formal communications that people consciously design and issue in some form; for example, publish, record, present, or put in memo form.

4. Messages are also generated through various computing devices and processes, and may be massaged, formatted, or organized by programmed instructions.

5. These messages are sought by or automatically routed to other persons who may or may not choose to make use of them.

These activities are included in what he referred to as value-added information systems. Taylor advanced the thesis that information systems, by virtue of their design, are value systems. Through the various processes (operations) that characterize such systems, the user's ability to access and select the information and knowledge that is available and required is facilitated.

Conclusion

This chapter has presented an overview of information system models by moving from a general theoretical framework to specific models and the concepts on which they are based. It first uses general systems theory to define the characteristics of a system; what it is and how it functions. This theory lays the foundation for describing types of information systems and the roles they play in our physical and social environment. From a different point of view, Churchman's model of a system centers on the human mind's natural curiosity. Intellectual inquiry is placed in the context of different philosophical perspectives. These perspectives can influence the design of information systems.

The structure of information systems is described by examining the biological systems model of Miller and the more generalized information system model of Debons. These models describe the components basic to all information systems.

The models of Otten, Heilprin, Yovits, Samuelson, and others are of a more specific nature. The full scope of any one of their models can be subsumed by one component of the general model of Debons. For example, Otten's model of an information system describes only the processing component of the model proposed by Debons.

Information systems can also be examined from the viewpoint of the users of the system. This viewpoint emphasizes the utilization component of the information system. Havelock's model thus describes an information environment, typically a library or information center. Taylor also refers to information systems as environments, and sees in their function activities that add value to the service that the system provides. These systems can therefore be seen as value-added information systems.

REFERENCES

Ackoff, Russell L., and Fred E. Emery. *On Purposeful Systems*. Chicago: Aldine-Atherton, 1972, 18.

Barnes, Robert F., Jr. "Information and Decision." In *Perspectives in Information Science*, edited by A. Debons and W. Cameron. Leyden: Noordhoff, 1975, 195-17.

Bertalanffy, Ludwig von. "General Systems Theory--A Critical Review." In *Modern Systems Research for the Behavioral Scientist*, edited by W. Buckley. Chicago: Aldine, 1968, 11-30.

Boulding, Kenneth E. "General Systems Theory--The Skeleton of Science." In *Modern Systems Research for the Behavioral Scientist*, edited by W. Buckley. Chicago: Aldine, 1968, 3-10.

Churchman, C. West. *The Design of Inquiring Systems: Basic Concepts of Systems and Organizations*. New York: Basic Books, 1971, 9.

Debons, A. "Command and Control: Technology and Social Impact." In *Advances in Computers*. Vol. 2, edited by F. Alt and M. Rubinoff. New York: Academic Press, 1961.

de Greene, K. B. *Systems Psychology*. New York: McGraw-Hill, 1970.

Harmon, Paul, and David King. *Expert Systems: Artificial Intelligence in Business*. New York: John Wiley & Sons, 1985, 49.

Havelock, Ronald G. *Planning for Innovation: Through Dissemination and Utilization of Knowledge*. Ann Arbor: University of Michigan, Center for Research and Utilization of Scientific Knowledge, Institute for Social Research, 1971.

Hayes-Roth, Frederick, Donald A. Waterman, and Douglas B. Lenat. *Building Expert Systems*. Reading, Mass.: Addison-Wesley, 1983.

Heilprin, Laurence. *Toward Foundations of Information Science*. White Plains, N.Y.: Knowledge Industry Publications, 1985.

Khailov, K. M. "The Problem of Systematic Organization in Theoretical Biology." Edited by W. Buckley. In *Modern Systems for the Behavioral Scientist*. Chicago: Aldine, 1968, 45-50.

Licklider, J. C. R. "Man-Computer Symbiosis." *Human Factors: Electron* 1 (1960):4-11.

McCormick, Ernest J., and Mark S. Sanders. *Human Factors in Engineering and Design*. 5th ed. New York: McGraw-Hill, 1982.

Machlup, Fritz, and Una Mansfield. *The Study of Information*. New York: John Wiley and Sons, 1983.

Miller, J. G. *Living Systems*. New York: McGraw-Hill, 1978.

Murdick, Robert G., Joel E. Ross, and James R. Glaggett. *Information Systems for Modern Management*. Englewood Cliffs, N.J.: Prentice-Hall, 1984.

Otten, Klaus W. "Information and Communication: A Conceptual Model as Framework for Development of the Theories of Information." In *Perspectives in Information Science*, edited by Anthony Debons and William J. Cameron. Leyden: Noordhoff, 1975, 127-48.

Samuelson, Kjell. "Information Models and Theories: A Synthesizing Approach." In *Information Science: Search for Identity*, edited by A. Debons and W. Cameron. New York: Marcel Dekker, 1973.

Scott, George M. *Principles of Management Information Systems*. New York: McGraw-Hill, 1986.

Shannon, Claude E., and Warren Weaver. *A Mathematical Theory of Communication*. Urbana: University of Illinois Press, 1949.

Taylor, Robert S. *Value-Added Process in Information Systems*. Norwood, N.J.: Ablex Publishing Co., 1986.

Whittemore, Bruce J., and Marshall C. Yovits. "A Generalized Concept for Analysis of Information." In *Information Science: Search for Identity*. Edited by A. Debons and W. Cameron. New York: Marcel Dekker, 1974.

5
Information System Technology

In this chapter we examine the technologies that are associated with each major component of the information system. Beginning with those that enable us to acquire data, we then discuss technologies that enable us to move data from one place to another (transmission technologies) and to process data (systems such as the computer). Finally, we discuss technologies that enable us to execute actions or convey meanings to others.

Of course, we can only cover part of the vast range of technology that we apply to information systems. The objective is to convey some general principles and provide some examples. The business of engineering and building information system technology is fast growing. Within a short time after the publication of this book many of the specific technologies will become obsolete, but the general principles governing their use will remain basically the same.

DATA ACQUISITION

Acquisition devices capture occurrences or events that may be of interest to the information system. Data can be digital or analog in form. Digital technology uses electrical impulses to represent the data according to the logic of binary arithmetic. Analog data are represented by rates of change in states of energy. A computer uses digital data. A telephone reproduces your voice in the analog form of sound waves; however, the sound may be converted to digital data for transmission through telephone lines and converted back to analog form by the receiving telephone.

Many acquisition technologies acquire electromagnetic energy in the form of light or sound; others sense heat and pressure.

The phrase *acquisition of data* is open to several interpretations, which are important for us to clarify. It may refer to *symbol acquisition*. If the events are represented by symbols, which are expressed in formal structures such as language, symbol acquisition is directly related to the context in which the symbols are embedded, be it a record, book, or classified document. Thus, symbol acquisition becomes acquisition of the document, report, or book.

Acquisition of data can also refer to the capturing of some of the actual energy generated by an event. We can refer to this kind of acquisition as sensory data acquisition. The application of technology to sensory data acquisition is based on an understanding of how our human senses acquire data from the external world, their capabilities and limitations, and how technology can augment these capabilities.

Human Aspects of Data Acquisition

There are a number of ways that humans can capture an occurrence or event. Nature has endowed us with senses that can sense energy and convey data about it through the central nervous system to the brain, where the data representing external energy is processed. Of course, our senses are limited in their ability to capture the event, particularly when the energy radiated is low or when the event is remote. For example, the unaided eye cannot see tiny bacteria or distant stars; we cannot see or hear structures and activities within living organisms. To enable us to capture these occurrences, we have microscopes, x-rays, and radio telescopes.

Signal-detection theory, developed by Swets and Birdsall (1978) and Tanner (1961), proposes that the direct capturing by a human of a signal in the form of energy is subject to a bias, which can be corrected by probabilistic analysis of the sensory functions involved. Signal-detection theory has its roots in psychophysics. It can be applied across the broad spectrum of considerations governing data acquisition.

Human factors engineering is the study of human physiology as it relates to the design of new technology. Physiological psychology is the study of the innate acquisitive capacity of the human mind.

Data-acquisition Devices

Much of the development of information systems can be related to rapid advances in electronics and electrical engineering. Many of these advances are in turn the result of significant advances in solid-state physics. It should be stressed, however, that information system structure by definition is dynamic and interactive, so a particular technology may serve several functions. For instance, data-acquisition devices may perform some processing to enhance the data received. The same transmission technology may carry signals both within and between components.

Data-capturing technologies may also rely on a combination of energy sources. For instance, radar and sonar use both light and sound energy, and at times pressure and heat as well.

Radar and Sonar

Two important data-acquisition devices are radar (radio detection and ranging) and sonar (sound navigation and ranging). Radar was developed during World War II by scientists in Great Britain who were confronted with the problem of detecting approaching German aircraft. The marine counterpart of radar is sonar. Both are detection technologies, their major function being to capture data about significant occurrences in the environment. Radar is particularly important for two reasons: (1) It can obtain data under many conditions (e.g., night, rain, fog, smoke, clouds); and (2) It is a significant means of measuring target range and direction, velocity, and size. Air traffic control, for example, is highly dependent on radar information in determining the position and movement of aircraft.

A major advantage of radar is its capacity for *remote sensing*. Remote sensing refers to the ability to capture events and occurrences at some distance. This is particularly important in detecting long-term environmental processes such as soil erosion or air or water pollution. Through the remote long-term gathering of electromagnetic radiation, we can obtain data on soil conditions, subterranean earth shifts that may give warning of earthquakes, and other events.

Satellites

Satellites can be either natural or artificial. Natural satellites are planetary bodies in orbit around other bodies in space. Artificial satellites are objects made and placed in orbit by humans. The objectives of artificial satellites can be numerous, but one of their primary functions is to acquire and transmit data. In space, they are able to receive and transmit signals otherwise blocked by the earth's curvature, its magnetic field, and its atmosphere.

Artificial satellites are a source of data about the nature of the universe, such as the shape and size of the earth, weather conditions around the world, conditions on other planets, and data about the magnetosphere. Manned space stations, a special type of satellite, may ultimately provide valuable scientific data.

Holography, Telescopy, and Photography

Glass lenses that refract light in specific ways provide another important form of data-acquisition technology. Several forms of technologies fall in this class.

Holography uses laser beams to record three-dimensional images on a photographic plate.

> Despite the fact that nature has provided man with an inherent capability to see objects in three dimensions through his visual systems, this capacity is lost and must be restored when mechanical means are applied. It is desirable for displays to depict three-dimensional data as such, because the recording of

objects on two-dimensional surfaces reduces the realism and quality of data. To retain this dimensionality in the acquisition technology, however, requires capabilities beyond what conventional optics can provide. Holography provides this possibility. Holography also permits the examination of large areas in three dimensions. In addition, holography provides the possibility of the study of a number of events which occur quickly. (Debons 1973)

Telescopy is a data acquisition technology through which distant objects are made to appear nearer and larger. A telescope is an optical device that includes two forms of energy processing, refracting and reflecting. Refraction occurs in two lenses: the eyepiece and the objective, a large convex lens. The reflecting element consists of a mirror.

Telescopy is a technology that for centuries has provided the basis for astronomy. During the past two or three decades, huge telescopes have been designed to search the universe to obtain data about the universe. Recent developments in medicine include the use of telescopes to probe the functions of several internal organs, including the heart, stomach, circulatory system, and the small and large intestines. Previously, medicine evaluated human anatomy through chemistry, often providing inaccurate data about physiological states. Telescopes, on the other hand, enable medical scientists and practitioners to examine the human interior.

A photograph is the product of light and chemistry. By combining the two in a mechanism (camera), an image is produced of an object or event. The image is transferred onto a chemical surface that is sensitive to light. In this sense, the camera serves as a data-acquisition device, while the film records and stores the data. Of course, photography transmits signals from one position in space and time to another, so it can also be considered a transmission medium.

DATA TRANSMISSION

Transmission is the movement of symbols or data from one place and time to another *without reference to the meaning or use of the symbols or data.* Of course, it is difficult to separate the signal from its meaning, but the important point is that transmission is governed solely by physical laws, while meaning is dependent on such factors as semantics, psychology, and context.

Shannon's Information Theory

The most influential theory concerning the transmission of signals was developed by Shannon (1949). His model of an information system derived from his work is discussed in Chapter 4. His basic formula is an attempt to quantify the movement of a signal through space and time. The movement is contained in a *channel*. The signal and the grouping of symbols or signal are referred to as a *message*. A message, according to Shannon's theory, is a physical (not a psychological) entity consisting of parts:

1. Reading: An indicator stating the initiation of a set of signals or symbols, when it was initiated, where it is to go, and to whom.

2. Body: Set of symbols or signs that contains the intention or purpose of the symbols. This segment presents the potential of the symbols to initiate a change of state in the receiver.

3. Conclusion or ending: A signature or a code indicating the termination of the message.

Shannon's formulation, expressed in mathematical terms, refers to quantitative aspects of the message as the impact of the signals or symbols on the receiver. The fundamental principle is that the message alters the state of the receiver in a precise manner. When the message is received, the state of the receiver is altered from *uncertainty*. This is expressed mathematically as follows: the degree of certainty gained corresponds to the number of symbols transmitted in the message.

Transmission Technologies

Advances in electrical engineering have provided a wide array of mechanisms for transporting signals and symbols. Of course, the need for such technologies began many centuries ago when humans found it necessary to convey their experiences and intentions to each other. The history of transmitting signals should not be restricted to humans, however. Other species have the capability to do the same, but with limited effectiveness; however, *Homo sapiens* has achieved significant advances in transmitting signals from one place to another, from the sophisticated use of light and sound signals, to Morse code, to the development of pencil, crayon, pen-ink, print, and, more recently, to technologies such as radio and television. Perhaps the most significant advance in transmission technology was the invention of the telephone. Although the telephone is basically a communication technology because it links users directly, it is an important way to transmit digital data as well as voice signals. Continuing advances in transmission technologies are further extending our ability to move from one place to another.

Laser

The term laser is an acronym for light amplification by simulated emission of radiation. Lasers produce a highly concentrated light source, far greater than is available from other sources. The importance of the laser as well as the maser (microwave application by the simulated emission of radiation) is that one can transmit signals over great distances with less diffusion or scattering of the signal.

Satellites

We have already mentioned satellites as acquisition devices. They also provide the capability to relay signals from other planets and stars and to transmit light and radio signals between earth stations at great distances.

Radio

Radio is a major transmitting device for sound signals. Little need be said about this familiar form of transmission. Like all transmission devices, radio is vulnerable to interference (noise).

Displays

Displays are media through which signals can be presented. They include the paper on which this book is written, highway signs, and cathode ray tubes, a device with which we are all familiar in the form of television picture tubes. Displays can be differentiated according to their function as transmitters.

Displays posted on highways to identify routes, recommend caution, and describe road conditions can be referred to as *static* displays or signs. The characteristic of a sign is that once written, it remains the same. Signs are influenced by environmental conditions (they age), and when they lose their effectiveness as conveyors of information they are replaced.

Dynamic displays, on the other hand, involve movement, or change, of the signal. Some move static elements mechanically, like the frames in a motion picture. The accuracy of the display depends on both the moving mechanism and the component images. Electronic displays are composed of dots, or pixels, which may be generated by electromagnetic radiation or liquid crystals. The state of the display at a given moment is determined by the combination of pixels, rather than by the selection of a particular frame from a set of static images.

Fiber Optics

One of the latest developments in transmission technology is the use of fiber optics. Optical fibers are very thin strands of highly conductive material that allow very fast propagation (transmission) of signal impulses. To the extent that such fibers produce a one-to-one representation of signals transmission, they are capable of higher resolution than other data transmission technologies. Fiber optics is an area that is experiencing considerable research and development attention because of its potential to revolutionize transmission and communication capabilities. Much of the research is focused on increasing conductivity characteristics, to lessen the requirement for power support to boost the signals for long-distance propagation.

Teleport Technology

Teleports are satellite transmission centers created to help revitalize the economic climate of large metropolitan areas by pooling local telecommunication resources. They represent a data transmission node analogous to an airport or railway terminal. Large disk antennas give them access to all the major United States and international communication satellites. Combined with sophisticated switching and routing capabilities and powerful receivers, a teleport allows instant worldwide transmission of signals. The teleport is linked by appropriate transmission technologies to businesses that subscribe to its services.

Cellular Radio Voice Transmission

Cellular radio technology provides personal mobile, cordless, long-range voice transmission. Cellular radio may eventually replace all current car telephones and walkie-talkies although expanded features such as conference calling and vis-o-phone will keep current telephone transmission in use. Cellular radio works by limited-bandwidth, low-power radio transmitters. This allows each channel to be used simultaneously in many geographic areas, as the individual signals are too weak to interfere with one another.

PROCESSING TECHNOLOGY

Processing technologies provide the means to analyze, categorize, and otherwise manipulate the data we acquire or transmit. Processing institutions, such as libraries, also pool the human data manipulation capabilities of many individuals.

Electronic Data Processing

Computer-based systems, sometimes referred to generically as electronic data-processing systems (EDP), vary widely in size, speed, complexity, and the applications for which they are used. Systems currently range from portable models that can be used while riding in a subway to large-scale, complex models that are custom-built for applications in weather forecasting, national defense, corporate management, and other uses that require thousands of person-hours to create and cost millions of dollars. Computers are becoming ubiquitous; they appear in everything from electronic typewriters to calculators to automobile engines and video games. They serve as electronic tellers, transmit mail and telephone calls, and operate machinery. Despite their diversity of uses, however, all computers do three basic things, the end result of which is the processing of data as opposed to information: they take *input*, or source data, perform predetermined electronic *processing* on it, and generate some kind of *output*, whether it be a bank account balance or a message to a robot arm controller.

Input may consist of any type of data--numerical, textual, or graphical. Humans enter input data from a variety of peripheral devices, the most common of which is the familiar computer terminal, with a cathode-ray-tube-based display screen and typewriterlike keyboard. Input also may come directly from another computing device via wires and microcircuitry.

Processing can be broken down into the basic steps of reading, adding, comparing, calculating, and writing. Processing is carried out by means of a program, a set of instructions to the machine that are written by human programmers. Complex programs are often composed of several smaller programs, combined in a specific sequence. Each of the component programs is designed to perform a particular function, such as providing an interface with the user or with other devices controlling the sequence of instructions to be executed, allocating memory space or other resources of the machine, or translating instructions from a human-readable programming language into machine-readable binary pulses. Programs are read from some input device or storage device to which the computer has access. They are loaded into memory, where their instructions are executed. It is possible for more than one program to reside in memory at one time on most computers, although the computer can execute only one instruction at a time.

Output is simply data that have been processed in some way, if only converted into some other form. Output can be in the form of a print-out on paper, a display of characters on a CRT screen, or a magnetic tape that is read by a computer as input for further processing. Other output devices generate signals for transmission over communications networks, create graphics displays, create microfilm images, or even mimic human speech.

Robotics

Robotics deserve special mention in this text for several reasons. First they are a fascinating and revolutionary use of computing and engineering technologies. Second, robots represent an excellent example of how technology can aid humans in performing highly complex tasks. Third, robots, unlike other processing technologies, have the potential to act on the environment itself and, through feedback, influence directly their own event world.

The Robot Institute of America defines a robot as "a reprogrammable, multifunctional manipulator designed to move material, parts, tools or specialized devices, through variable programmable motions, for the performance of a variety of tasks" (Logsdown 1984).

Actually, robots are processing technologies that are sometimes intended to replace, rather than augment, the motor functions included in work operations. Logsdown (1984) referred to them as "teleoperators with microprocessors for brains." Robots have been gaining in popularity because of their usefulness in hazardous environments, such as the handling of nuclear wastes and toxic chemicals where the process and materials involved would represent a danger to human operators.

Robots present a real challenge to mechanical engineers as well as to computer scientists. Although the early work done on prosthetic devices provided considerable expertise in the development of parts for robots, the engineering of flexible joints

97

remains a challenge. The matter of developing computer programs that drive the robot is a difficult and exacting process requiring precision to capture the essence of movement.

In recent years the robot has become a focus of artificial intelligence research. The ultimate aim of robotics is to create a machine that is self-sufficient and adaptive to various conditions (both stable and changing) of the environment. To accomplish this, knowledge about sensory processes in general and visual processes as they relate to pattern recognition becomes vital. These considerations consume the attention of theoreticians and engineers alike (Feigenbaum and McCorduck 1983).

Processing Institutions

Up to this point we have briefly sketched the machine technologies that process data as an essential function of an information system. The library is an *institution* directly linked to the processing of data, information, and knowledge. As the custodian of knowledge, the library serves as a major resource for the storage and retrieval of data, information, and knowledge. Thus, the library is an essential component of many information systems, equally as important as the technologies. As Carl Sagan, noted scientist and communicator has suggested in a CBS documentary, the library may be considered as analogous to the human brain in function.

Information Analysis Centers

An information analysis center (IAC) is a system operating at the highest level of intellectual sophistication relative to the storage and retrieval of knowledge. Such a center maintains a staff of subject specialists who perform the analysis function. The analytical processing of data input (books, reports, tables, statistics, etc.) involves the manipulation of ideas and concepts, and the relationships among them. The output of the analysis consists of these derived relationships and logical deductions about them. Often new information and knowledge is produced from such analysis and manipulation.

As early as 1963 the President's Science Advisory Committee recommended the growth of these specialized information centers Therefore, most IACs are in federal agencies where specially filtered and categorized information is needed by scientists and engineers, or in the public domain at large institutions such as the National Aeronautics and Space Agency (Weinberg 1963). The Weinberg report emphasized that

> knowledgeable scientific interpreters who can collect relevant data, review a field, and distill information in a manner that goes to the heart of a technical situation are more help to the overburdened specialist than is a mere pile of relevant documents. Such knowledgeable scientific middlemen *who themselves contribute to science* are the backbone of the information center; they make an information center a technical institute rather than a technical library. The essence of a good technical information center is that it be operated by highly competent working scientists and engineers--people who see in the operation of the center an opportunity to advance and deepen their own personal contact with their science and technology. Proliferation of the specialized information centers will therefore require many such "information scientists": dedicated and knowledgeable technical men who help interpret and assimilate the literature for others working in the field.
>
> The specialized information center is a technical institute, not a technical library, because its staff knows the contents of the material held by the center thoroughly. Basically, the staff members are scientists, although they use the tools of librarians. What is retrieved from such a center is not documents, but information. (Weinberg 1963)

An IAC attempts to use all of information channels to provide technical answers to technical questions. Although it must spend money and effort on acquisition, storage/retrieval, and analysis, typically 80 percent of the budget is spent on paying for the expertise of the staff.

REFERENCES

Augarten, Stan. *Bit by Bit: An Illustrated History of Computers*. New York: Ticknor and Fields, 1984, 295.

Debons, A. "Holography and Information Sciences." In *Encyclopedia of Library and Information Science*. New York: Marcel Dekker, 1973, 10:456.

Feigenbaum, E. A., and Pamela McCorduck. *The Fifth Generation: Artificial Intelligence and Japan's Computer Challenge to the World*. Reading, Mass.: Addison-Wesley, 1983.

Lin, Nan. *The Study of Communication*. Indianapolis: Bobbs-Merrill, 1977, 29.

Logsdown, T. *The Robot Revolution*. New York: Simon and Schuster, 1984, 18, 19.

Richardson, Ernest Cushing. *Classification: Theoretical and Practical*. 3d ed. Hamden, Conn.: Shoestring Press, 1964.

Sayers, W. C. Berwick. *Manual of Classification for Librarians and Bibliographers*. 5th ed. Revised by Arthur Maltby. London: Deutsch, 1975.

Shannon, Claude E., and Warren Weaver. *A Mathematical Theory of Communication*. Urbana: University of Illinois Press, 1949.

Simpson, George A. "Microcomputers in Library Automation." *Mitre Corp. Technical Report* 7938 (December 1978):21-25.

Swets, J. A., and Birdsall, T. G. "Repeated Observation of an Uncertain Signal." *Perception and Psychophysics* 23 (1978):269-74.

Tanner, W. P., Jr. "Psychological Implications of Psychophysical Data." *Annals of the New York Academy of Science* 89 (1961):752-65.

Weinberg, Alvin M. *Science, Government, and Information: The Responsibilities of the Technical Community and the Government in the Transfer of Information, a Report of the President's Science Advisory Committee*. The White House, 10 January 1963. Washington, D.C.: U.S. Government Printing Office, 1-52, 260.

6
Communication Technology

A person's effectiveness often depends on his or her ability to convey meaning and ideas to others--in a word, to communicate. In this century, conventional ways of conveying ideas by paper and pencil or photographs have been supplemented by sophisticated transmission technologies that have improved our ability to convey meaning to others more quickly and directly.

WHAT IS COMMUNICATION?

A term that is synonymous with communication in the literature is *information transfer*. One can refer to data transfer and knowledge transfer in this context as well. Information transfer can be defined as the process of extending a state of awareness and related intentions, singularly or plurally, to others. Data transfer, by contrast, denotes the transmission of symbols, which may or may not have the power to inform. Knowledge transfer is the conveyance of understanding, perhaps the highest form of communication.

Lin (1977) provided an extensive treatment of the various aspects of human communication. She stressed that the *act* of communication should be separated from the *discipline* of communication: "Communication [is] a scientific field in which the

103

nature of human symbolic exchange is studied." If we consider information transfer to be the act of alerting (making aware) individuals to the state of the event world, we can then ask: what processes does this involve and what technologies contribute to it? For communication to occur, there must be at least the physical capacity to transmit the signals, but beyond that, let us consider the aspects of awareness as the effect of communication.

The act of being aware is fundamentally a cognitive function. First, it requires that we use our senses to acquire data and to transmit a representation of it to our brains. This process is the first step toward awareness. Thus, if the objective of information transfer is to make other persons aware, an important requirement is that the signals that initiate the process must be of sufficient energy to be received. A weak auditory or visual signal may not lead to awareness, and thus information transfer will not occur.

Second, if the signal received by the individual for whom it is intended cannot be decoded, the full intention of the signal may be lost. An individual may not be able to decode a signal, but may still be *aware* of it. The conveyance of meaning is an essential element of information transfer. If meaning is not preserved, no information transfer has occurred. What may have occurred, where symbols are received but they do not inform the receiver, is data transfer.

In addition, information almost always occurs embedded in context. The context may be as important as the symbols being transferred to the information content of the signal. Spoken and written language sounds, sights, data of all kinds must be received in context to transfer their information content.

With these introductory comments on communication, let us attempt to survey briefly the technologies that are important to it, keeping in mind our distinction between those related to transmission and those related to communication.

The communication technologies that we will briefly survey are displays, film, print, spoken language, and networks and telecommunications. In addition, we should examine the institutions that have incorporated these technologies and provide services that are part of communications and information transfer, such as the media, educational institutions, libraries, and news services.

Visual Communication Technologies

Electronic Displays

Electronic displays are vital transmission technologies. They are also primary communication technologies. The television is just one example of the importance of electronic displays in communication among human beings. The electronic display is also the primary source of interaction between data processing technology and the user. It is the key interface in the man-machine link.

Film and Photography

Film is an important means of communicating events, whether for record-keeping, recreation, art, or instruction. Continual advances in film technology have significantly improved its usefulness as a means of communication. New production processes have led to greater resolution (clarity) of figures and symbols and the decay of films has been substantially delayed. New processes have also reduced the time for developing film while substantially improving the quality of the image. Corresponding advances in technology have increased the efficiency and effectiveness of cameras. These developments provide greater realism in depicting events, and at a lower cost in both human effort and money.

Print

Perhaps the most significant advance in communication technology in the last 500 years was made by Gutenberg, a German printer who lived in the early part of the fifteenth century. He revolutionized the world's communication capabilities with his introduction of the *printing press*. This provided for wide distribution of data about events and ideas that formerly were transmitted only by individually transcribed printed materials or by word of mouth.

A major contemporary development in the communication technology has been the process of *xerography*, which allows print to be duplicated through chemical and thermal processes.

105

Facsimile printing is another technology that enables the transmission of data by sending a digitized image of the data over cable-transmitting devices. In addition to documents with graphic elements, fingerprints and pictures of missing or wanted persons are important uses of this technology.

Language

Of course, language is an important form of communication technology. Some might object to referring to language as technology, but indeed it is a manmade construct, enabling us to deal with the world. Language comes in numerous forms, each of which reflects the history, ideas, and habits of a culture.

Language can be expressed visually, as on paper or an electronic display, orally, by hand signs, and even by smoke signals. Each of these forms reflects the diversity and complexity of language structure.

NETWORKS AND TELECOMMUNICATIONS

There is a powerful trend in our nation and throughout the world toward the development of computer networks based on sophisticated communication technologies such as telephones, satellites, television, and radio for the purpose of improving the use of our knowledge resources. *Telecommunications* is directly related to the development of such capabilities. One of these communication services is a commercially available subscription that gives access to data bases containing on-line media on everything from home improvement to baseball box scores.

Another is independent electronic bulletin boards, which offer informed group-oriented files of correspondence and ideas on everything from acquiring software to home shopping. These systems are usually set up by some interested person or group who takes the responsibility of buying and maintaining the software needed to run it. Participation is fun and, one hopes, informative, and usually solicited by word of mouth (in a digital sense!). Access requires little more than dialing a telephone number.

Data Communication--Technology and Technique

Data communications (as opposed to voice communications) unquestionably have had a tremendous impact on business, government, education, and even home life. Within the past ten years, communication of data over telephone lines has grown at a far faster rate than any aspect of voice communications. Data communication networks (which consist of some kind of transmission system, plus computer hardware, communications interfaces, and controlling software) can send data across a building, across town, or across the world. Often, a small computer, a modem (a signal converter that lets you send digital signals over phone lines), and the right telephone number are all that are needed to subscribe to stock quotation services, electronic bulletin boards, or time-shared computer time on a variety of systems almost anywhere on earth. Despite their great diversity of size and scope, nearly all networks stem from a few basic configurations and are often controlled in very similar ways.

Networks

A network consists of some kind of transmission medium, such as the existing telephone lines, and the hardware and software needed to control the flow of data within the network. The topology of a network refers to the physical configuration of its various nodes. A node refers to a computer and/or its peripheral devices, or any other point at which data going out differ in form or content from data coming in. A telephone is a node in the local telephone network, for example, because incoming voice transmissions stop at it instead of propagating beyond it, and new signals generated there flow along the open line in the opposite direction. Nodes in a data communication network function in much the same way, responding automatically to signals from one another through the software that drives them.

A network design is extremely complicated, involving such considerations as perceived needs for speed and flexibility, combined with cost, maintenance, and existing technologies.

Data Transmission Technologies

The bottom line in transmission technologies (often referred to as telecommunications) is bandwidth, or the amount of data a given medium can propagate, without error, from source to destination. Five basic technologies are in use today for the purpose of transmitting data between nodes of a data communications network. Two of these, satellites and microwave technology, require the transmission of waves through the atmosphere (or even from space) from source to destination. The other three make use of some kind of cable or waveguide to link network nodes directly.

The three basic types of direct-connect technology are the twisted pair of copper cable, used for both voice and data transmission; the coaxial cable, which provides sufficient bandwidth to allow voice, data, and video to be transmitted simultaneously (thus making possible cable television); and fiberoptic cable, a material that supports very high-frequency waves (of 10-100 gigahertz), is tap proof, is nonflammable, and rarely short-circuits.

Microwave transmission involves very short radio waves of 1 to 100 cm. Unlike conventional radio waves, however, their range is only about 25 to 50 miles, after which their reliability drops rapidly as errors occur. Microwaves traveling over long distances must be rebroadcast by a series of repeater stations, which strengthen their signal and filter some types of errors. Microwaves are reliable and have a wide bandwidth.

A satellite is a kind of radio tower in the sky. Satellites serve as relay points from which earth stations with special antennas rebound signals. Traveling up to 22,300 miles above the earth, most satellites move in an orbit that exactly matches the rotation of the earth. This is referred to as geostationary or geosynchronous orbit. Earth stations using a satellite in geostationary orbit point their dish antennas at the same location in the sky at all times. Each system can effectively transmit to one-third of the earth's surface.

Satellites use solar-powered repeaters (called transponders) to do the job of earth-bound repeater stations. A transponder receives a signal at one frequency, boosts its power, and rebroadcasts it at a different frequency. If security is to be maintained, all these signals must be scrambled and sorted out again "earthside."

Satellites are excellent, or course, for the one-way distribution of data. A video signal from a cable television station requires some 2400 voice channels on each transponder. Satellites are often the only way to broadcast such high volumes of data across long distances.

Other uses for satellites include radio broadcasts, video teleconferencing (employed by some hotel chains and by large professional organizations), and the transmission of facsimile sheets of typeset pages from national newspapers to their printing plants.

Cable Television

Cable television differs from regular broadcast TV in four major ways: it has expanded channel capacity; it makes possible two-way communication; it is easily combined with other media such as telephone and radio, and it has more diverse special interest programming.

Communication and the Professions

Our educational system, the library, and media of journalism and television are professions that serve as important information transfer or communication agents. In this volume we can allude only to some of the factors through which communication technologies influence their function.

Charles J. Sippe (1976) defines media as "a general term referring to printed matter." We can add to this definition: a general term referring to displays and related technologies whose objective is to provide a vehicle for the transmission of data, information and knowledge.

Educational Media

Educational institutions are a primary means in transmitting knowledge from one generation to another.

David Hawkridge (1983) discussed the difficulty at arriving at a consensus as to what constitutes information technology in education. He cited the extended definition by UNESCO. According to David Raitt (1982), it consists of

> the scientific and technological and engineering disciplines and the management techniques used in information handling and processing; their applications, computers and their interaction with men and machines; and associated social, economic and cultural matters.

This definition makes a number of assumptions. Reference is made to information, management techniques, and social, economic, and cultural matters. But Hawkridge provided a more direct definition of such technologies that we can align with education. He identified computers, micro-electronics, and telecommunication as falling within this class of technologies.

Computer-Aided Instruction (CAI)

This form of communication technology attempts to use the computer as an adjunct to (not a replacement for) other instructional tools and methods. The format and sequence of conceptual ideas/data are developed in a program that allows students to interact with the computer at their own pace.

Electronic Blackboard

This communication technology has direct application to education. It provides the capability of multiple transmission of material from one primary blackboard source to others located elsewhere. This enables the instructor to instruct students in remote locations.

Home Video

Television sets can be used for instruction at home. Hooked up to bidirectional cable, the student at his home can proceed at the desired pace in studying a course. This form of technology often includes instructors who serve as consultants on specific areas of subject difficulty. The student who encounters a particularly difficult segment of the course dials a telephone number that connects the student with an instructor, who then provides help on that point.

The Library

The library as a communication channel provides access to a number of services and resources. Among those presently available is the access to on-line data bases through time-sharing systems, such as DIALOG, ORBIT, and BRS. Through this capability the user is able to search and retrieve references in the form of citations and abstracts and then decide what additional sources are required. Sometimes the source material resides in the library collections and is readily available. If not, the library can access the resource-sharing network to which it belongs and that is made up of member libraries whose materials are available on loan to the requesting library. Online Computer Library Center (OCLC) is such a network on a national scale, enabling nationwide sharing of material resources. The Library of Congress lends to other libraries if no other library contains the needed item. It is the library of last resort.

With the advent of more and more on-line catalogs in individual libraries, the user can access the holdings from a terminal. The card catalog still exists, but because of the low cost of micro- and mini-computers, more and more libraries are putting bibliographic data in machine-readable form. The most common record is the MARC formatted record of the Library of Congress. This national library catalogs and classifies millions of items, committing the bibliographic data to magnetic tape that can then be disseminated to other libraries for a fee.

Message center programs by libraries are also becoming increasingly common, as is on-line availability to users of community data and community information locations for referrals. A community can have resource files on clubs, government agencies, adult education, day-care centers, career and occupational data bases, and community events, which shows the scope of such possibilities (Bohl 1980).

There is a growing demand for information and materials by computer disk or optical videodiscs. Optical discs are capable of storing entire books. If the optical disc is coupled with the appropriate computer interface, the user could scan an entire work, printing out only what is needed (Dowlin 1980).

Electronic mail is ideally suited for interlibrary loan activity, newsletters, and memos. Easy-Link is a Western Union system that allows libraries to use electronic mail for interlibrary loan transmission; it also offers worldwide electronic mail delivery (LITA 1985).

Retrieval from a library collection is effected by means of the library's catalog, which most likely is on-line and thereby searchable on a computer terminal. Most systems allow the searcher to search by title, author, subject heading, ISBN (international standard book number), and LCCN (Library of Congress catalog number). Many also allow Boolean searching. The data base must have been indexed by assigning terms, identifiers, or descriptors to represent the content of documents. With an indexing language to describe contents of textual material, the searcher thus chooses the appropriate term or terms for the machine to search. It is on the matching of the input terms to the terms in the index and the subsequent identifying of the documents having such terms assigned that "hits" are made.

Journalism

News is new information about anything; information previously unknown; reports of recent happenings, especially those that are broadcast or printed in a newspaper. In attaining its objectives, journalism uses all of the data acquisition, transmission, and processing technologies previously discussed in this chapter. The following are technologies related to specific journalistic functions.

Editing and Reporting

The newspaper editor's function is complex and diverse. It requires up-to-date acquaintance with related facts that may be of interest in reporting an event. Thus, the editor must have quick access to historical data. This can be provided through the use of a data base specifically tailored to chronology, personalities, and historical events. The *New York Times* data base has been designed to aid the editors and the reporters in their task of reporting the news.

Distribution

Many newspapers and news periodicals (magazines) are intended for national or international distribution (e.g., the *Wall Street Journal, Newsweek*, the *New York Times*). Facsimiles, where one issue of the paper can be transmitted over cable or by satellite, provide an important capability in transferring news over long distances and to a larger population of readers. *USA Today* uses satellite communications to relay the contents of each edition to presses all over the country, allowing simultaneous printing and availability.

Conclusion

This chapter makes an important distinction between transmission of signals and the act of communication or information transfer. Information transfer takes place within and between minds or information systems. This transfer of information is an act of communication. Communication technologies are media that enable transmission of data or signals between minds of information systems whose intent is to communicate.

Communication technologies that facilitate transmission of signals are, for example: film, printing, language, television, the telephone, the satellite, microwaves, and magnetic media. When these media are interconnected by means of some design, as in a telephone system or cable television system, the result in general terms is called a network.

Telecommunications technology is usually found in combination with institutions such as libraries and with professions such as journalism and education. Each of these employs many different media to help effect information transfer.

113

REFERENCES

Bohl, Marilyn. *Information Processing.* 3d edition. Chicago: Science Research Associates, 1980.

Dowlin, Kenneth. "The Electric Library." *Library Journal,* 1 November 1980, 2266.

Hawkridge, David. *Information Technology in Education.* Baltimore: Johns Hopkins Press, 1983.

Heilprin, L. *Toward Foundations of Information Science.* City Knowledge Industry Publications, 1985.

Lin, Nan. *The Study of Communication.* Indianapolis: Bobbs-Merrill, 1977, 29.

LITA *Newsletter,* no. 20 (Spring 1985).

Raitt, David. "New Information Technology--Social Aspects, Usage, and Trends." In Proceedings of the Fifth International Online Information Meeting, London, 8-10 December 1981, edited by Lucy Tedd et al. Oxford: Learned Information, 1982.

Sippe, Charles J. *Data Communication Dictionary.* New York: Van Nostrand, 1976, 293.

7
Information System Synthesis

The extent to which an information system can synthesize information from data determines its ability to solve problems. The capacity for synthesis is the single most important factor in the success and viability of any information system, whether organismic or organizational. This chapter discusses ways in which systems analysis and design determine the capacity of information systems to achieve synthesis.

WHAT IS SYNTHESIS?

Synthesis is the combination of separate elements into a whole that is more complex than the sum of the parts taken individually. J. G. Miller, in his treatment of living systems, considered the ability to synthesize data input to be a fundamental characteristic of all living systems:

> Processes--usually logical in nature--are carried out to diminish available alternatives to a lesser number characterized by the ability of decreasing to a satisfactory degree the deviation of the state of the system from the comparison signal. This makes possible survival of the system while keeping costs of the necessary adjustment process reasonably small. (Miller 1978)

To Miller, synthesis implies the maintenance of a steady state while directing the system toward its goal. Synthesis comes about through processing of the inputs collected from throughout the system. Implied in this is the concept of control--maintaining system stability for efficient and effective achievement of objectives.

An information system must synthesize the data it acquires about events so that its output is not merely data but information. A living system must process data and become informed for the sake of its survival. An information system made up of humans and technology together must provide information to meet its objectives. The goal of the systems analysis and design processes is to maximize the extent to which the system can synthesize data into relevant forms that enhance awareness, that inform us rather than confuse us or inundate us with data.

Information systems consist of interacting elements. It is their ability to interact coherently that provides the core of an information system's ability to synthesize data to obtain information. The physical boundaries of an information system are the spatial and temporal forces making up the environment in which the system exists. The environment includes the institution or organization in which the system is embedded, along with its inherent social structure and belief system. Events are occurrences representing changes in the state of the environment that the information system is designed to capture. Events emit energy that, when captured, provides the basis for formalized processing of signals so that they can be recorded, stored, and retrieved.

Processing occurs within several components or subsystems of the overall information system. Each subsystem individually and collectively provides the capacity for the transformation of the energy emitted from an event (represented by data) to other forms of energy that can affect human consciousness, leading to awareness.

The essential objective of information systems is to provide awareness of events to ensure survival. Survival may be restricted to the range of applications to which artificial information systems can be applied, such as in the economic survival of an organization. Survival also can be interpreted as encompassing a wide range of human activities and aspirations. Information systems provide data, information, and knowledge required to support problem solving and subsequent action.

System Design and the Capacity for Synthesis

The capacity of an information system to synthesize data and provide information is rooted in the design of the system. Artificial information systems are designed, so to speak, by their environments. Both artificial and living information systems must evolve apparatus for acquiring and processing relevant data before they can perform synthesis and move towards their respective goals. For artificial systems, relevant inputs must be defined and means found for acquiring them. Rules and procedures must be set up for processing these inputs and applying them to problems and decisions. The ability to synthesize data and provide information is at the heart of any functioning information system.

These tasks are addressed by the activities of systems analysis and system design; activities that are themselves examples of the capacity for synthesis on the part of living systems that the artificial information system must emulate.

Analysis and design can be seen as two consecutive steps in the same process. *System analysis* refers to the examination of an activity, procedure, or organization to find out what must be accomplished to meet objectives and how the necessary operations may be best accomplished. *System design* is the creation of a detailed plan of the architecture or structure of a system.

In this book we have asserted that although a system consists of components, these components are systems in and of themselves (usually referred to as subsystems). This concept implies that systems and their components always represent a hierarchical arrangement (Miller 1978). Quite often, analysis of a component of an information system is suggested to represent the analysis of the entire information system, leading one to conclude that the component is an information system in its own right. This mistaken reference can obscure some fundamental properties that differentiate the functions of a component of an information system from the greater information system it serves. For example, analysis

117

of a computer as a component of an information system may aid us in designing a particular part of the system. In considering processing needs, however, we must also take into account transmission requirements, for example, and how they will affect the design of the processing components. A given computer may meet perceived data processing needs, but the addition of sufficient access ports to support the transmission network may degrade performance below acceptable levels. The computer is not the whole information system; it is only a processing component.

The process of systems analysis can be directly linked to the model that is used as the basis for the analysis. In other words, the conceptual model of the system determines the scope of the analysis. Because so many models of systems are described in the literature, different conclusions for systems analysis arise from each one. The literature, however, provides much more agreement on the parts of an information system than may be apparent at first. In fact, it is often more difficult to determine the differences among models than it is to determine the similarities. For example, the input-throughput-output model is the most fundamental of all information system models, whether the treatment deals with the computer as a component of the system or as the information system itself. Also, the user is a component of almost all system models. Similarly, almost all models and theories agree that an accurate account of data from the environment is an important aspect in the design of an information system. There are numerous perceptions as to how such components (data processing, user, environment) are to be handled, however, and what aspects are to be emphasized and deemphasized. Some would like to stress the role of language (semiotics) in the assessment of the environment (Pearson and Slanecka 1977), others the legal, budgetary, or social constraints on a system.

Strategies for Systems Analysis

C. West Churchman (1971) detailed the various aspects that can be considered to represent systems thinking: (1) objectives of the total system together with performance measures; (2) the system

118

environment; (3) the resources of the system; (4) the components of the system; (5) the management of the system. The following synopses of system analysis strategies highlight the basic similarities and differences among approaches.

Schoderbek's Approach

P. P. Schoderbek and his colleagues define systems analysis in terms of five factors: formulation--clarifying, defining, and limiting the problem; search--determining what data are of relevance; explanation--building and testing a model; interpretation--deriving conclusions; and verification--testing these conclusions by experimentation. The next step in the process could be designing of a system based on these conclusions. This approach emphasizes the inductive process, in that it moves from specific inputs to a general design strategy (Schoderbek, Schoderbek, and Kefalas 1985).

Neuman's Approach

Neuman (1982) emphasized a less experimental, more deductive form of reasoning. Here, the present system is analyzed to define the dynamics occurring within it. A determination is made as to what the user's information requirements are and why the present system cannot meet them. This determination forms the basis for the design of a new system.

Miller's Approach

Perhaps the most elaborate conceptual scheme for system analysis provided to date is that proposed by J. G. Miller (1978) based on a biological metaphor for an information system, and structured on several basic characteristics of all living systems. These include the components that were presented in Chapter 4 when we discussed Miller's model. The assumption is made that system analysis should include an understanding of the underlying dynamics that constitute the basic structure of each component. A successful systems analysis can only be achieved when the various (numerous) hypotheses that are generated regarding the properties and functions are experimentally defined, supported, and subsequently verified.

Debons's Approach

Debons presents a variation of Miller's model. Also using the living organism as a metaphor of an information system, he proposes that information system analysis must be approached by applying theories, laws, and principles from various disciplines, thus giving information science (whose major interest is the structure of such a system) its interdisciplinary character. Like Miller's, Debons's view of system analysis is reductionistic and empirical. From the fundamental structure that is provided (EATPUT), each of the components and its respective laws and principles can be presented in the form of a matrix. The blocks of the matrix should be filled in by specifying the principles, laws, and theories that now relate to the definition and structure of each component. The entries in the blocks represent those principles that are now known to relate to the component and that therefore should be included in the system analysis process.

It is important to state the essential difference between the Miller and Debons conceptualizations. Whereas Miller concentrates more on the properties and functionality of each discrete subsystem or component of the system, Debons stresses the need to integrate hypotheses about the related functions that enable the system to reach its homeostatic state. The Miller and Debons approaches are not mutually exclusive in their conceptualization of information systems analysis and synthesis.

Friedman's Approach

Another variation of a conceptual scheme, one that is probably more conventional than that proposed by Miller or Debons, is presented by Friedman (1975), sociologist and information scientist. His analysis is componential in character, but its similarity to an overall information system can be readily appreciated. Friedman develops the analysis procedure into several stages, some of which allude to design.

Stage 1: Investigation and definition of user problems; requirements and obligations of current operation; organizational policies, goals, plans, configuration, etc., as well as the development of a design specification and description of system benefits.

Stage 2: Mapping of organization and potential users, delineation of application and performance benefits and their operational definitions; development of systems concepts; design of system operational requirements (hardware, software, and humanware) in terms of application and performance benefit definitions.

Stage 3: Implementing system design requirements--system development and operating phase.

Stage 4: Conducting experimental evaluation program to test three subjective hypotheses concurrently. (a) The operational capabilities of system components will meet performance criteria and show improved performance (the performance tests). (b) The attained performance capabilities will accomplish the required application benefits (the application tests). (c) The achieved performance and application benefits will improve user mission accomplishments and slow the necessary system benefits (the mission tests).

Friedman developed this concept by proposing several postulates:

1. A discrete integrated system ensemble (component) is always a part of a larger system.

2. The components of a system are extended integrated functions of a larger system.

3. A single component is continually in an active state before, during, and after the advent of a specific stimulus or an operation on related and nonrelated internal and external stimuli.

4. The system is bounded by the time considerations that influence each of the preceding postulates and related variables.

One should note that many of the same concepts occur in each of the approaches discussed.

Mandates for Analysis and Design

System analysis is always focused on the question of "How should it be done?" Mandates serve as useful tools for analysis and design because they are often the result of experiences of practitioners who either as system analysts or system operators have dealt with the reality of constructing, operating, or maintaining systems. In the final analysis, the creation of information systems with the ability to provide synthesis results both from those who are concerned with what information systems are and from those who are concerned with how information systems work or do not work.

Kent's Approach

An early contributor to the thinking on information systems, Kent (1966) proposed the following factors to be included in their design:

1. Objectives: The overall purposes of the system.

2. Functions: Major classes of actions or performance required to achieve the objectives.

3. Performance requirements: Specific dimensions of required actions, with a statement of the standard or required level of performance for each.

4. Environmental variables: Properties of the environment that affect the system and its performance.

Zimmerman's Approach

Zimmerman (1983) examined a number of information system design models, analyzed the weaknesses of each, and produced some prescriptions for systems design:

1. The goals of the system must be completely and precisely defined. From this a design will logically follow.

2. The initial representation of the problem is the most important step in the development of a solution.

3. The nonrational, creative aspects are critical components of the design process.

4. For carefully selected variables, a hard decision-making technique, such as cost-benefit analysis, can significantly reduce the number of remaining variables about which decision must be made.

5. A priority list of design tasks is helpful.

6. Performance-evaluation techniques must be built into the system from the beginning.

7. Some form of performance evaluation to collect performance data is needed.

8. A final design must be preceded by some form of dynamic model of the system.

9. A poorly designed system can result in hostile behavior by users, which will eventually obstruct and frustrate the most sophisticated design.

10. The process of identifying and dealing with conflicts is critical to a successful system design operation.

Martin's Approach

J. G. Martin (1984) believes that in the practice of good system analysis one should:

1. Automate the system analysis method as much as possible.

2. Avoid using manually devised charts of information flow and the like, but use the computer to develop these charts.

3. Develop ways to automate the generation of codes.

4. Tie in the data-administration process to the analysis.

5. Avoid ambiguity.

6. The process should be documented by computer processing procedures rather than by hand.

7. Bring the user into the analysis process.

8. Build prototypes.

9. Use structured techniques that are user friendly, that rigorously automate verification checks, and that provide sound data administration.

Conclusions about Analysis and Design

There are other prescriptions for performing information system analysis--too many to include in this account. Despite what seems to be an array of different concepts, whether at the overall or component level, there is agreement on the basic structures, processes, and functions included in an information system.

Robert Hayes (cited in Borko 1967), in summing up the principle of system analysis, wrote:

The one thing characterizing the entire process--from definition to design to evaluation--is repetition and modification. As a result of the analysis new requirements will be defined and objectives changed. Some desires are not feasible and must be reduced, and the attempt to define alternative solutions will reveal analysis gaps. So the steps outlined above [problem definition, selection of objectives, analysis, definition of alternative solutions, evaluation, iteration, and reiteration] do not represent a simple sequence, but rather a complex, iterative, dynamic process. The result [of the analysis] is a system design including a complete description or "documentation" and a plan for implementation and conversion and with sufficient flexibility to accommodate later changes.

SYSTEM DESIGN AND SYNTHESIS CAPACITY

In our attempt to understand the information system's capacity for synthesis we may now ask, how does system design contribute to the synthesis we are referring to, namely, bringing components together into an efficient, effective functioning entity for human purpose? Debons and Larson (1978) differentiated design as a process and as a product, citing the fact that design is an output, while designing is the process leading to the output (Swanson 1974). Borko (1967), an information scientist, distinguished the design process from the analysis process: "*System analysis* is a formal procedure for examining a complex process of organization, reducing it to its component parts, and relating these parts to each other and to the institute as a whole in accordance with an agreed upon performance criterion. *Systems design* is a synthesizing procedure for combining resources into a new pattern."

Note Borko's use of the phrase "synthesizing procedure for combining resources into a new pattern." This suggests that the process of information and knowledge synthesis as it takes place in design may indeed be a creative process born out of insight and intuition as well as hard work. The question of whether design is a science or an art was raised by over 100 scientists who attended a conference in Crete in 1978 sponsored by the Scientific Affairs Division of the North Atlantic Treaty Organization (Debons and

Larson 1978). Science and art were concluded to be similar processes, but differences were noted. While science is dedicated to predictability, art is dedicated to form. The designer is often a distance apart from his creation. The designer receives feedback much later in the process than the artist, who is the immediate receiver of his or her creation. There are differences of a formal nature as well. The designer as a scientist is bound by the constraints of the paradigm of his peers (and sponsor) in the formulation of the design. Artists, on the other hand, are held to their own visions rather than to external requirements. Artists modify their creation as they see fit and as they move along, the restrictions being part of their own perceptions and values. Most designers are seldom given such a free hand. The degree to which the artist is subject to external constraints is different from that imposed on the engineer, but both must synthesize diverse inputs creatively to achieve their goals.

The point we wish to stress is that the business of design is *applying or implementing the results* of the analysis process. Often the analysis process is confused with the design process. Given the analysis of what is wanted and needed, we must next determine what the resources (hardware, software, persons, power sources, etc.) are that we can bring to the design to construct an information system. Of course, our primary interest, as we have indicated previously, is to determine how these processes taken together enable the integration of the components into a cohesive whole.

Designing for Interaction among Components

Quite often the requirements dictated by analysis determine whether existing hardware can meet the new design specifications. An ever-advancing state of the art for software as well as for hardware leads to revised system specifications for such technology. Integrating new technology into the system requires that the designer carefully probe the nature of the interfaces between processes within the system. The design is akin to introducing a new heating system into a house as the result of energy-conservation requirements. The home designer must review architectural properties of the home to the extent that other aspects (e.g., insulation, vent location, interior-exterior object movement) are consistent with the addition of the new system.

Costs incurred in acquiring resources and applying them to the system often dictate design, forcing accommodations and assimilation, which compromise the system synthesis potential. Thus we return to our need to acquire a new heating system for our home. To take advantage of reduced use of energy (cost), we must readjust or accommodate our living habits (movement, level of satisfactory heating levels for our comfort) to meet the desired level of energy use (cost). We have to incorporate (assimilate) these new habits in our daily routine. These adjustments are part of the design process. Trade-offs always must be made.

It is necessary in the design process to adjust and calibrate the functioning of the system components so that they are fully integrated. The inclusion, for instance, of a new computer with updated capabilities in terms of input, throughput, and output requires a detailed analysis of its relationship to existing components, such as data transmission and display capabilities. The practice of molding the user to the system works the other way as well, because quite often hardware and software specifications are reconsidered in light of user feedback.

Synthesis of Individual System Components

As we indicated, the information system consists of a number of components (acquisition, transmission, processing, utilization, and transfer) (see chapter 4), each contributing to the overall functioning of the system. Each of these components, along with the event world, can be considered subsystems of the overall system. The design of individual system components can be aided by certain theoretical formulations. These ideas provide a framework for design.

Event World

For events to be captured, they must on some level be classified and categorized. Although classification and categorization theories deal with the ordering of knowledge, they can have broader application with respect to determining ways to *represent* events. Classification of knowledge is of great interest to librarians. Scholars of artificial intelligence are equally concerned with representing events by formalizing the structure of data so that it ultimately can provide the basis for the development of intelligent systems. An event can be dissected into three parts: actions, relations, and properties. These can be represented by words in a *script*. The dynamic properties of the event are then developed into a *scenario*.

An example of application of classification-categorization theory that is relevant to event world analysis concerns the structuring of data in a computer data base. How data are structured in the computer for ultimate use depends on adequate identification and labeling, and on the relationship among the critical elements of an event.

Acquisition

Of primary importance in capturing events are the limits of human sensation and perception. Both have been dealt with extensively by physiologists and psychologists, and understanding the technical aspects requires detailed study and cannot be treated adequately here. Information systems often employ sophisticated sensor technology that greatly exceeds human data acquisition capacities, like radar, sonar, the optical lens, and x-rays. The effectiveness of both human and technology-based acquisition components is dependent on the nature of the system that reflects the event and the receiving mechanisms that capture it. Also, the relevant data received must not be overwhelmed by unusable data (noise), and must not be in quantities so large that the transmission or processing components are overloaded.

Transmission

Transmission, the movement of signals and symbols captured from an event, is the concern of *transmission theory* (which includes code theory). In the human body, neural mechanisms move stimuli (or energy) from an external source through the neural network and ultimately to the brain. From the technological perspective, electronics and particularly information theory (as developed by Shannon [Shannon and Weaver 1949]) provide the theoretical framework.

Processing

Three types of processing apparatus are of primary importance: the central nervous system and particularly the brain, which processes data from sensory elements; the computer, which is a data processing technology; and the library, which is the reservoir of sources representing the record of human experience.

The brain has been studied extensively in attempts to uncover the processes that directly or indirectly contribute to our awareness (consciousness) or to our knowledge (Minsky 1975). The transmission of energy (as represented by stimuli) through the central nervous system to the higher centers of the brain is represented by several models and theories provided by physiologists, particularly neurologists (McCulloch and Pitts 1943). These theories are important to information scientists because they provide for an understanding of the limits of human performance that should be accounted for in the interfaces linking people and technology in information system design. These theories are also used by cognitive scientists (Simon and Newell 1978) in their attempt to understand how data are processed in learning, memory, thinking, and perception. Understanding these processes is essential in the development of knowledge systems (knowledge engineering).

The library represents a processing element of an information system, because it receives, classifies, categorizes, stores, and retrieves the records that are contained (packaged) in media (paper, film, etc.). The underlying framework that supports the processing function of libraries is *classification theory*, previously mentioned. Classification functions are the bases of *information-retrieval theory*, which attempts to establish the relationship between the logistical (storing and retrieving) aspects that govern documents with the needs (utilization) of users.

Utilization

The broad range of theories relating to learning, thinking, memory, and language, can be applied to the analysis and design of the utilization component of information systems. Historically, decision theory and probability theory (Edwards 1954) were most influential in this area, along with game theory, risk analysis, and crisis management. These efforts provide a basis for present work (Simon and Newell 1978) in artificial intelligence where understanding of how humans process data can be used to develop decision-making, problem-solving models for computer application. An important part of such work is the attention given to language (Schank and Birnbaum 1980; Chomsky 1965), particularly to sentence structure (parsing), semantical analysis (meaning of words in a sentence), and knowledge representation through language. Much of the theoretical work that directly applies to utilization of information is based on the assumption that humans are limited in their capacity to process complex data correctly and to process large volumes of data quickly.

Transfer

The term *transfer* is often used as a synonym for *communication* or *dissemination*. Transmission is a necessary (but not sufficient) requirement for transfer. Transfer is the conveyance of meaning or significance, derived from what others have experienced and represented by some action. Information transfer can be differentiated from knowledge transfer. The differentiation is a matter of degree rather than of kind. Information transfer aims at making others aware, while knowledge transfer extends this awareness to higher cognitive levels (understanding and synthesis).

Theories abound for each of these aspects of the transfer component.

Shannon's information theory is important to any discussion of transfer owing to its reference to the message, which is the critical element of the transfer function. Although Shannon's theory provides an account for the transmission aspect of the transfer process, it fails to provide a comprehensive theory of communication that integrates concepts of transmission of messages with measurements of significance or meaning. Several theories are concerned with how transfer occurs. One is proposed by William Goffman (1970), who applies the disease metaphor to the communication process. Given a description of how disease can be communicated to others, Goffman developed mathematical formulations that account for such processes.

Some social factors underlying transfer are: issues of confidentiality and privacy, and the influence of technology and media on behavior and dissemination of information. Previously, the library was discussed as part of the processing function of the information system. The library as the custodian of the record of human experience serves as a communicator, a disseminator of such experience. In its role as intermediary, the library brings accumulated knowledge to the user through its human and technological resources. Through the social structure it integrates these resources.

Applying Design Ideas from Other Disciplines

Cybernetics, ergonomics, and management science represent different ways of applying the systems approach. Each provides a framework for integrating or synthesizing the components of the information system into a cohesive whole.

Cybernetics

Cybernetics is a diverse field encompassing (1) integration of communication, control, and system theories; (2) development of systems engineering technology; and (3) practical applications of hardware and software. Recent and projected developments in cybernetics are taking place in at least five important areas: technological forecasting and assessment, complex systems modeling, policy analysis, pattern recognition, and artificial intelligence.

The formal principles of cybernetics can be briefly summarized in the following propositions:

1. A system and/or its components undergo transformations as a function of time. Any system is in a constant state of change as it attempts to adapt to changing environmental conditions. Of course, nonliving systems and components require human intervention to change in positive ways, with few exceptions. The alternative to adaptive, positive transformation is performance degradation leading to a cessation of function (Wiener 1971).

2. All components of a system must deal with the data they receive at any given time. A component's state therefore is the condition of a component that can be described based on information that component possesses about its own state and the state of other components. The formalism that governs these concepts is referred to as information theory (as previously discussed) and deals with the degree of noise (entropy) in the system and the reduction of uncertainty.

3. It is possible, through an understanding of data load and the degree to which that load fluctuates, to generate a series of mathematical equations relative to the activity between component boundary layers that will provide a measure of the influence of feedback on system performance.

Information scientists can apply the basic principles of cybernetics to the integration of components of an information system.

Ergonomics

Ergonomics is the study of the role of human beings in (1) the design and creation of man-made objects, products, equipment, facilities, and environments; (2) the development of procedures for performing work and other activities; (3) the provision of services to people; and (4) the evaluation of the functionality or ease of use of a technology.

The principle of ergonomics or human factors is directly relevant to information system design and analysis. It is through the application of principles relating efficiency and effectiveness through work (and other human activities) that the various components of an information system can achieve their goals.

Ergonomics includes the study of the role of displays in human activities, human control of systems, the use of technology in human and system functions, and physical space and environment. Each of these will be briefly discussed to highlight important considerations for the analysis and design of the information systems.

The Role of Displays in Synthesizing Information

Displays are essentially transmission devices. They act as conduits in transmitting data from either the acquisition component to the processing component, or from the processing component to the user. They serve as a vital element in the communication or "information transfer" function as well. They also serve as feedback devices, providing vital data concerning the consequences or results of a particular action that has been taken by the user or the system. In this role, the display provides the basis for the user to monitor the functioning of the various parts of the system. When displays incorrectly or inefficiently provide data regarding the state of the system, dire consequences to the entire system may result. The

Three Mile Island incident demonstrates the importance such technology played in the overall functioning of the system. Perhaps because displays were secondary to the design of the overall information system, they proved to be inefficient in predicting circumstances leading to a nuclear accident. Christopher D. Wikens (1984), an ergonomist, provides an account:

> Within a minute after the original shutdown, the supervisory crew at Three Mile Island was attempting to understand what was going on from a myriad of alarms, lights, and signals on massive display panels. Though their training allowed them to capture a fairly accurate picture, they were led astray by one signal. The display for the pressure relief valve was designed to indicate what the valve was commanded to do rather than what it actually did, and the display indicated that the pressure relief valve had closed.
>
> It is interesting to note that no display was designed to indicate what the valve was doing. Through a series of human errors what could have been merely a minor incident turned out to be a near-catastrophe.

Human Control of Systems

Human control of systems acts to synchronize the various parts of an information system by means of the following factors:

1. The *ability to respond* (reaction time, latency) to change in the state of the environment through the various components of the system. This is a form of adjustment behavior where measures of both human and technological states are used to balance stabilizing forces or counter-forces. The ability of machines to respond is reflected in the design specifications accompanying the technology. The ability of the human to respond effectively to states is measured by methods from the disciplines of sensor physiology and psychophysics. (Psychophysics is the study and measurement of the capability or capacity of sensor systems to respond to energy.) The ability of the entire information system to

work in synchrony is often greatly affected by the design characteristics that account for these two human variables.

2. The *act of responding* (decision making, problem solving) to alternatives that are made evident by the state of the information system.   A delay in responding to a contingency will influence the data flow throughout the system.   Systems requiring human response must be designed so that the range of possible responses all are well within the range of human capability.   Operators must be able to perform error correction, balancing, and criteria adjusting.   Delays in the processing and presentation of data affect these capabilities (Crossman 1955).   Information systems are vulnerable to control errors because of the delays with which data are presented, thus influencing the effectiveness of prediction and anticipation. The initiation of action by the system can induce a lag in the feedback loop. This action leads to what could be referred to as a blackout (a period in which no data are available).

Technology in Human and System Functions

As indicated previously, technologies are extensions of human abilities. Tools and devices are used to control, as well as initiate, processes. The skills with which tools and devices are used direct the level of functioning of respective components of the systems. Numerous ergonomic principles have been derived that quantify the performance of humans in various control functions; the reader is directed to several ergonomic texts (McCormick and Sanders 1982; De Greene 1970; Wikens 1984; and others). It is relevant to our purpose to show how such principles serve as factors in creating information systems, to indicate several fundamental principles regarding the role and design of tools and devices in the information system design process.

Accounting for the *structural anatomy* of the human organism in the design of tools and devices is directly related to the efficiency that is possible in the use of that technology as an element of the human-machine interface. This is a fundamental characteristic of all information systems. For example, a computer keyboard characterized by nonstandard key spacing that does not account for hand anatomy cannot be used efficiently.

When tools and devices are directly linked to data processing capabilities, the extent of the input and output of such devices must correspond to the *level of difficulty of the task* (Fitts 1954).

In the use of tools and devices in information system design, provision should be made for the development and or *updating of skills* (training) corresponding to the characteristics and functions of such devices.

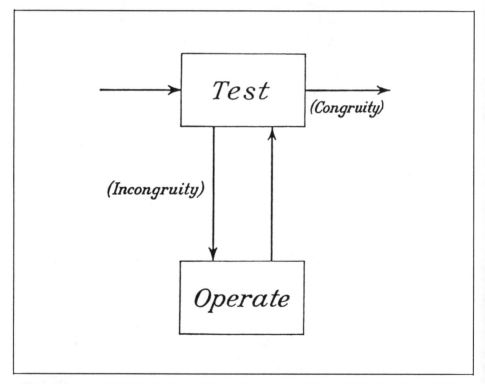

Figure 7.1. The TOTE Unit. (From Miller, Galanter, and Pribram 1960. Reproduced with permission.)

Feedback is a highly critical element in the use of tools and devices. Perhaps the most succinct illustration of the principle is presented by G. A. Miller, K. H. Pribram, and E. Galanter (1960). Galanter's model is concerned with the feedback action associated with a series of sequential actions, each playing a role in forming a plan of action. This concept of a plan of action based on testing for individual discrete events or conditions is related to the total range of possible actions or "operations" involved in the system. The "test-operate-test-exit" (TOTE) method of monitoring a condition can be applied to a wider frame of reference, to show how tools and devices function, and to integrate a number of operations (see fig. 7.1). For example, TOTE feedback loops control your car's fuel mixture and engine temperature, as well as mammalian body temperatures and the feeding behavior of flies.

Physical Space and Environment

All information systems, whether human or a combination of human and technological, occur in physical environments. Proper lighting, noise levels, temperature, and so forth serve to improve the functioning of the system's human components, thus making possible the function of the whole system.

The placement of a particular component of a system (e.g., radar, display, computer) is limited by its physical size. Physical size could effectively influence (positively or negatively) the use of that particular component in the overall system.

Each system component, through its characteristics and operating specifications, defines the limit of the interfaces that are possible with other components.

All components of an information system are inherently influenced by available power sources and the fluctuations that can be expected from such sources. Accounting for such fluctuations can enhance system synthesis as much as ignoring them can lead to poor performance.

The human as the vital synthesizing component of a system is highly influenced by the available light, the atmospheric conditions (heat, cold, humidity), noise, and other disturbances. When system analysis does not account for these factors, the system design will be less than optimal, negatively influencing the functional harmony among the various system components.

Management Science

Management science is the study of concepts relating to the planning, controlling, operating, and directing of human and technological resources in organizations.

Management science can play an important role in providing a synthesis of the various theories and concepts underlying the components of an information system. In attempting to develop a statement on the education of information professionals, Buckland (1982) provokes us to see some of the signs of synthesis that can be achieved:

1. The growth of knowledge will demand increased efficiency and effectiveness of information systems through their relevance to institutional and individual functioning. Greater attention will be paid to their integration into organizational structure, thereby demanding that each of the components of the system functions well in relation to each other and to the whole.

2. The information system will be seen as an integrated whole and not solely as a computer-oriented, computer-based system. Attention will be paid not only to the access and transmission and processing of data but also to the ability of the system to serve as a source for analysis and in general, the development of knowledge.

3. Trained professionals in the system will know the ins and outs of the system, enabling refinement of component functioning and component interfaces. The fact that trained people with diverse educational background and professional interests will be brought together to operate and manage such systems will increase the possibility of

developing different and rich concepts about how information systems operate as a whole.

REFERENCES

Borko, Harold, "Design of Information Systems and Services." In *Annual Review of Information Science and Technology*, vol. 2, edited by C. A. Cuadra. Washington, D.C.: American Society of Information Science, 1967.

Buckland, Michael K., and E. H. Boehm, eds. *Education for Information Management: Direction for the Future*. Santa Barbara, Calif.: Information Institute International Academy, 1982, 14-16.

Chomsky, Noam. *Aspects of the Theory of Syntax*. Cambridge, Mass.: MIT Press, 1965.

Churchman, C. West. *The Design of Inquiring Systems: Basic Concepts of Systems and Organization*. New York: Basic Books, 1971.

Crossman, E. R. F. W. "The Information Capacity of the Human Operator in Symbolic and Non-symbolic Control Processes." In *The Application of Information Theory to Human Operator Problems*. Proceedings of a special technical meeting. London: Ministry of Supply, Great Britain, 1955.

Debons, A., and Arvid Larson. "Information System and Design in Context," in *Information Science in Action: System Design*. The Hague: Martinus Nijhoff Publishers, 1978.

De Greene, K., ed. *Systems Psychology*. New York: McGraw-Hill, 1970.

Edwards, W. "The Theory of Decision Making." *Psychol. Bull.* 51 (1954):380-417.

Fitts, P. M. "The Information Capacity of the Human Motor System in Controlling the Amplitude of Movement." *Journal of Experimental Psychology* 47 (1954):385.

Friedman, Lee. "The Measure of a Successful Information and Storage Retrieval System." In *Perspectives in Information Science*. Edited by A. Debons and William Cameron. Leyden: Noordhoff, 1975, 383.

Goffman, William. "A General Theory of Communication." In *Introduction to Information Science*, edited by Tefko Saracevic. New York: R.R. Bowker, 1970, 727-47.

Hayes, Robert. "Library Systems Analysis." In *Data Processing in Public and University Libraries*, edited by John Harvey. Combined proceedings of the Drexel Conference on Data Processing in Public Libraries, 22-23 October 1965, Philadelphia, Pennsylvania. Washington, D.C.: Spartan Books, 1966, 5-20.

Kent, Allen. *Textbook on Mechanized Information Retrieval*. 2d ed. New York: Interscience Publishers, 1966, 275.

King, Donald W. *Key Papers in the Design and Evaluation of Information Systems*. White Plains, N.Y.: Knowledge Industry Publications, 1983.

McCormick, E. J. and Mark S. Sanders. *Human Factors in Engineering and Design*. 5th ed. New York: McGraw-Hill, 1982, 4.

McCulloch, W. S., and W. T. Pitts. "A Logical Calculus of the Ideas Immanent in Nervous Activity." *Bull. Math Biophys.* 5, (1943):115-33.

Martin, J. G. *The Information System Manifesto*. London: Prentice-Hall International, 1984.

Miller, G. A., E. Galanter, and K. H. Pribram. *Plan and Structure of Behavior*. New York: Holt, 1960.

Miller, J. G. *Living Systems*. New York: McGraw-Hill, 1978.

Minsky, Marvin. "A Framework for Representing Knowledge." In *The Psychology of Computer Vision*, edited by P. H. Winston. New York: McGraw-Hill, 1975.

Neuman, A. *Principles of Information Systems for Management.* Philadelphia: Wm. C. Brown Co., 1982.

Pearson, C., and V. Slanecka. *Semantic Foundations of Information Science.* Atlanta: Research Rep. School of Information Science, Georgia Institute of Technology, 1977.

Schank, Roger, and Lawrence Birnbaum. "Memory, Meaning, and Syntax." Report 189, Yale University, Department of Computer Science, 1980.

Schoderbek, Peter P., Charles G. Schoderbek, and Astevios G. Kefalas. *Management Systems.* 3d ed. Plano, Tex.: Business Publications, 1985.

Shannon, Claude E., and W. Weaver. *The Mathematical Theory of Communication.* Urbana: University of Illinois Press, 1949.

Simon, Herbert A., and Allen Newell. *Human Problem Solving.* Englewood Cliffs, N.J.: Prentice-Hall, 1978.

Swanson, R. "Design and Evaluation of Information Systems." *Annual Review of Information Science and Technology* 9 (1974):25-59.

Turing, A. M. "Computer Machinery and Intelligence." *Mind* 59 (1950).

Wiener, Norbert. *Cybernetics, or Control and Communication in the Terminal and the Machine.* 2d ed. Cambridge, Mass.: MIT Press, 1971.

Wikens, C. D. *Engineering Psychology and Human Performance.* Columbus, Ohio: Charles E. Merrill, 1984.

Zimmerman, Patricia J. "Principles of Design of Information Systems." In *Information Science in Action*, edited by A. Debons and A. Larson. The Hague: Martinus Nijhoff Publishers, 1983, 30.

8
Social and Moral Issues

The sharing of awareness and understanding is a sociological phenomenon. Information and knowledge sharing is a collective, group enterprise. The enterprise exists within a social structure, the function of which is control and innovation (Havelock 1971). By *social structure* we mean the supporting institutions, the functional elements and their related activities, including policy formulations, that ensure the survival of the society. Information systems in social structures are the instruments through which the social entity, whether it be the family, group, city, state, or nation, receives the awareness required to maintain its position among other similar entities.

INFORMATION AND SOCIETY

Manfred Kochen, in highlighting and summarizing his views about information and society, stated (1972):

> The world's people are and should be increasingly well informed about significant societal changes that are likely to affect them: the threat of nuclear war, labor displacing technologies, and the differences between the qualities of life that could be and that exist. Economic, political, social, and educational institutions

depend increasingly on information and are involved in its production. Dilemmas demand resolution: the need for strength to make us more secure while the danger of misusing that strength makes us less secure; the need to increase productivity when the means for doing that displace more jobs than they create; the need to please when we don't know enough to plan; the scarcity of needed information amidst a glut of information.

Centralized versus Decentralized Information Systems

Information systems may be located at different levels within the social structure, and their role will vary according to the level. The power of information systems is exerted through the filtering of data throughout the group, influencing the status of many components of the group. When information flows from the top level, the management function exercises *control* through its ability to change or manipulate the states of individuals at lower levels, by controlling the degree to which they are aware and informed.

The social issues and considerations regarding centralized control of information flow can be summarized briefly as follows (Debons, Mitchell, and Furdell 1967):

1. What are the differential benefits to be accrued from centralization when it is clear that it deprives the lower levels of the awareness of events that is necessary for them to do their job effectively?

2. What is the function of middle echelons of a structure under the information-poor conditions that centralization invokes?

3. Can the social structure be preserved in conditions of information centralization?

Distributed-Nondistributed Processing

Distribution of data reflects decentralization of data processing, while nondistribution of data indicates that the data processing is done at the top level of a social structure. Technologies such as telecommunications favors distributed processing. Lias (1982) claimed that distributed data processing, which established a decentralized form of social structure, ultimately will be subject to centralized control. In other words, there will be multiple data-processing centers throughout the structure. Whether such individual autonomy will enhance the functioning properties of the social structure is a question that must be addressed by those who are now contemplating such distributed centers as part of their telecommunication plans.

The Social Value of Information

In many ways, information is seen in the same sense as oxygen--it is freely available. Its importance is realized only when the user is deprived of it. Nations use information and knowledge as resources. These resources and their benefits should be available to all citizens equally. Without accepting or denying the worth of such a philosophy, practical realities demand that free access be considered as part of a means of knowledge storage and retrieval. Information and knowledge for their own sake must certainly aid the development of individuals and ideas. The aggregation of information and knowledge for specialized purposes that lead to profit may be another matter. The critical issue is the *worth of information*. This issue has been the subject of considerable discourse and analysis by information scientists. Donald W. King (1980), an economist and information scientist, has compiled papers from various scholars to provide a basis for understanding a number of issues.

The cost of information products and services is arguably the most pervasive economic problem in the information field today. One major question that has emerged is whether or not to charge for information products and services, particularly those that are partially funded by the government. The answer to this question relies at least partly on external events, such as the social benefits of the information to society. Both the information content and availability affects external events and determine social benefits.

Establishing the value of information is the most complex aspect of the economics of information. The complexity is compounded by theoretical difficulties, such as defining information content and the benefits derived from information, as well as empirical difficulties, such as determining an appropriate unit of measurement for information. Evaluating the value of information requires relating supply costs to demand benefits, the results of which are reflected in pricing or some other type of measuring mechanism. Thus, the definition of information in economic terms is particularly crucial in this context since it is the information content that ultimately yields value or social benefit.

One of the more complicated problems to overcome in placing a value on information is relating the use of information to the value derived from that use. Attempts have been made to define this relationship. For example, the economic properties of information may be different from those found in other economic goods and services. Moreover, a true cost and benefit comparison has yet to be made. The traditional economic approach to analyzing information as a marketable commodity is perhaps meaningless.

The Cost of Information Research and Development

The cost of information systems analysis and design is usually amortized by the corporation, government, or, at the lowest level, individual. The corresponding worth of information systems is often measured in terms of their *perceived value*. The importance of information that is incomplete or poorly distributed is very often not recognized. Thus, the crucial phases of information systems analysis and decision may be compromised by inadequate resources.

Privacy and Centralized Information Storage

The acquisition and correlation of personal data, now in numerous computerized files and data bases, has stimulated concern for privacy and confidentiality. Information systems tend to increase the production and availability of data about both groups and individuals, thereby increasing the potential for control of groups and individuals. Private data about individuals is now subject to public access. Privacy is linked to confidentiality, but their meanings are distinctly different. Confidentiality suggests that some subject matter may not be disseminated to others because it would compromise secrecy about a particular business deal, military strategy, etc. Privacy refers to limits on public access to individual personal data.

Privacy and confidentiality can represent conflicting goals and outcomes. For example, our Constitution helps to ensure that we have free and ready access to important data by protecting our rights to free speech and a free press. The Freedom of Information Act passed by Congress in 1973 addresses this objective in the United States so that the citizen is always aware of important national news and information. On the other hand, such actions lead to potential violations of privacy and deter confidentiality. In the words of the Rand Report (1974), "Society demands economy, efficiency, and an high degree of utility from public agencies. This is in conflict with the subject's demand for confidentiality, and restrictions in the use, dissemination and sharing of data."

Information control implies that there are ways of restricting individual awareness of relevant events. The reasons for restricting awareness of events may be public or private. A nation may not wish the public to be aware of how it will confront a potential enemy. A company may wish to keep information about an invention away from competitors. John Doe may not wish to have his financial situation and spending habits known. The converse may also be true. For example, the United States may wish to publish reports on its military strength as a potential deterrent to hostile action. John Doe may wish to alert everyone of his wealth so as to influence his status in the community. Information control implies the ability both to disseminate and to withhold information.

Censorship

Censorship is a form of information control in that it attempts to restrict a dissemination of selected materials or other data. Censorship influences numerous areas of human interest and enterprise. Directly or indirectly, censorship attempts to restrict individual or public access to subject matter that may be considered objectionable (e.g., sex in general, or books or films on controversial subjects) (Daily 1973). In modern terms, censorship is an attempt to regulate the flow of data through the media (television, radio, newspapers, etc.). It can be argued that government intervention in the structure and economics of communications (networking) would impede the independent dissemination of information, particularly with respect to news. The television medium shares common ground with radio, journals, newspapers, and all media in which censorship and government regulation pose a serious threat to freedom of the press and to the public's right to know.

Copyright Law

Questions concerning the dissemination of information have arisen because of the technology of computers and photocopiers and have taken on a new and complex structure. Because the means are now available for quick and easy copying and disseminating of documents, persons who wish to obtain knowledge are claiming the right to use these means to procure the documents they desire. At the same time, those who produce information, such as authors and publishers, are claiming the right to be compensated for the materials they rightfully own. Under the present copyright law some feel that this right is being infringed upon. The debate touches all levels of the academic community, the judicial system, and the knowledge industry in general. It appears that what is needed is an examination of the underlying structure of the knowledge creation process and the rules and laws that govern the flow of information. Basic questions that should be evaluated are: Is free flow of information necessary in the generation of new knowledge? Does the existing copyright law provide an impetus for researchers to generate and record knowledge or information? Do new technological developments, such as computers and photocopiers, stimulate or inhibit the dissemination of information and growth of knowledge?

Collectivism

One of the foremost exponents of extending our capabilities in dealing with data, information, and knowledge beyond national borders is Manfred Kochen. He has been a fervent spokesman for the development of a "world knowledge system." He believes that a major concern of information science is to determine how knowledge can be distributed and accessed worldwide, and that people need to have access to knowledge if they are to maintain a reasonable quality of life (Kochen 1972).

The ability to be aware of current events in any part of the world is possible only for a fraction of the world's population. People in only a small number of nations can receive up-to-date news coverage of world events from radios and televisions. Although the situation is improving thanks to satellite communication, many societies and cultures can be said to be impoverished in the amount and kind of information they receive. It is important to recognize that the present international communication (transmission) system determines the information that people in many countries receive. Of course, the ability to transmit and receive data is (as is often the case in the United States) independent of the relevance, timeliness, or information content of the data.

Literacy Rate

The greater the literacy rate in a society, the greater the demand for printed material. An indictment of international proportions is the fact that over 25 percent of the world population is illiterate. Although many of these individuals manage their lives quite satisfactorily, the quality of their lives must often by compromised by the inability to read or write their native language.

The ability to read and write in one language is a requirement for the use of nearly all information systems. Individuals who have access to information systems benefit from understanding the limitations and capacities of the technology at their disposal.

Poverty

For many individuals who live under conditions of poverty, awareness of the world is limited to the local area in which they live. Only free materials are available to them, and these are often generated by agencies that may be politically motivated. Thus the information they receive may be slanted to achieve specific ideological and economic objectives.

Language Barriers

Multiplicity of spoken languages in some countries hinder communication, particularly in developing countries. Translation resources are limited and, when available, expensive. Much data, information, and knowledge are available in only one language, often English.

Transmission Channels

Developing countries have fewer transmission channels over which to receive and transmit messages, news events, and other data. This applies to the transmission and receipt of messages from overseas as well as internally.

Wire services disseminate most international news. Developing countries often cannot afford the offices required to process such services as well as the subscription rates that such services demand. Many possess outdated telecommunication capabilities. In an attempt to ensure that adequate dissemination resources are available to various countries, UNESCO (1976) has established minimum standards for communication media. They require that the country involved have a minimum of ten daily newspapers, five radio stations, two television stations, and two motion picture establishments per one million people. Many countries fail to meet these standards.

Political Establishments

Embassies and consulates are established to ensure communication between countries on many important aspects of social and cultural interaction. A disparity exists between developed and developing countries where the latter cannot afford the expense of embassy staff and facilities. Thus, developing countries have fewer embassies with smaller staffs, again limiting the exchange of information.

Information dissemination is critical to the task of running any institution or society. Information is truly power when it comes to taking appropriate action to safeguard security--be it the security of an individual, a company, or a government. The present state of affairs for developing countries is that most of them are faced with information deprivation. Decision makers in these nations function in an isolated communication world, separate both from each other and from those in the developed, more powerful countries. They lack the quantity and diversity of data they require to be informed about the world. In addition, they lack necessary feedback about the actions they take. It is possible that such countries may rely on information supplied or filtered from developed countries, information that may compromise the interest of such countries.

The Social Impact of Information Technology

Each technological development in the history of human evolution has influenced the species to some extent in one way or another, positively or negatively. Many sources in the literature of information science provide assessments as to the impact an information system has had or could have on the social structure. Debons and Larson (1983) stated:

> Impacts may be considered to be the result of an event or process which causes, gives rise to or produces change. Impacts are the result of the induction of a particular system on the social structure. When judgments are made regarding the impact of a

151

particular system in the field, we are in effect evaluating the operational quality of that system. Thus, an understanding of the impacts of information systems is part of the evaluative process in system design.

Impacts of information systems on the social structure are suggested to be of three kinds (Debons and Larson 1983):

1. *Immediate impacts*:   Quick reaction to system characteristics that may lead to the acceptance or rejection of the system in whole or in part.

2. *Short-range impacts*:   These are impacts that can be anticipated in the near future. Changes in organizational hierarchy or work flow often stem from the recent introduction of information systems. These changes in turn influence the systems.

3. *Long-range impacts*: These impacts are projections based mainly on factors involving the lifetime of the system. Global trends involving white collar professionals working at home as a result of the introduction of personal computer networks is an example.

Alvin Toffler's *Future Shock* (1970) and *The Third Wave* (1980) are particularly significant sources. Toffler, a journalist, captures the ramifications of the psychological and social impacts of the "information age." Some of these impacts include (Toffler 1970):

Overstimulation of the individual through information received and action required as a result of the availability of data and knowledge. The ability of the senses to respond to stimulation is limited.   By classifying information, abstracting and coding data in various ways, we manage to stretch these limits. Too much summarization limits the value of data, however.

Society demands that we make faster decisions, while at the same time reducing their possible negative consequences.

This leads to decisional stress. Toffler (1970) indicated some of the consequences:

a.   People tend to deny reality or certain aspects of it.

b.   Individuals are forced to narrow their range of interests in order to deal with life effectively.

c.   People regress, doing things that were previously enjoyable or easy, but that are no longer significant or worthwhile.

People become "super-simplifiers," reducing their understanding of an experience to its simplest dimensions.

One aspect of information science that has received some attention is that of the role of media in shaping the perceptions and attitudes of individuals. The late Marshall McLuhan has been highly influential in stressing the effect that mass media, such as television and radio, have had on the individual. McLuhan (1964) stresses the difference between "cold" and "hot" characteristics of media. Hot media have a direct appeal to every receiver; they provide a complete simulated sensory experience and evoke similar thoughts and emotions in all who are exposed to them. Hot media are "filled with data" (data here meaning the sheer physical/sensory impact of media rather than their potential informative content). McLuhan calls hot media "noninvolved" because they are "low in participation" on the part of the receiver. A sexy car commercial exemplifies such a medium.

Cool media, conversely, are disguised and reserved. The receiver must fill in aspects of his or her personal experience to compensate for real or implied gaps in both meaning and sensory image, making the transfer of both data and meaning individualized and different for every receiver. Cool media demand an "analytic act" just to acquire or receive them; they are "involved"--low in sense data but "high in participation" for the receiver. Good political satire, for example, falls into this "cool" category. McLuhan and Fiore (1967) claimed that:

All media work us over completely. These are so persuasive in their personal, political, economic, aesthetic, psychological, moral, ethical and social consequences that they leave no part of us untouched, unaffected, unaltered.

Information systems are part of the social structure of all governments and institutions: local, national, and international. Directly or indirectly they impinge on the individual and collective identity--at times threatening the integrity of the individual and group as well. They provide the means for control by restricting individual and collective awareness. They become part of the commerce of ideas through practices that regulate the distribution of knowledge. On a more positive note, however, they provide for a greater collective awareness and understanding.

Greater awareness and understanding are positive forces, but they are not without consequences. The world becomes smaller, neighbors more visible. The impact of events is direct and ideological perspectives are more vulnerable to abrupt changes. These conditions cause humans stress and anxiety. With further developments in technology will come greater collective consciousness. The social and moral question is whether this enhanced consciousness truly improves the quality of mankind's collective existence.

REFERENCES

Boorstin, Daniel. *The Discoverers*. New York: Random House, 1983.

Booth, Wayne C. "The Company We Keep: Self-Making in Imaginative Art, Old and New." *Daedalus* 3 (Fall 1982):33-60.

Cavell, Stanley. "The Fact of Television." *Daedalus* 3 (Fall 1982):75-96.

Daily, Jay E. *The Anatomy of Censorship*. New York: Marcel Dekker, 1973.

Debons, A., and A. Larson, eds. *Information System in Action: System Design*. Vol. 1. The Hague: Martinus Nijhoff, 1983.

Debons, Anthony, Robert Mitchell, and William Furdell. *The Effects of Automated Data Processing on Naval Command*. Naval Research Laboratory, Technical Report, Washington, D.C., 1967.

De Grolier, Eric. "Some (More or Less) Philosophical Thoughts on Information and Society." In *Perspectives in Information Science*. Leyden: Noordhoff, 1975, 631-658.

Havelock, Ronald G. *Planning for Innovation*. Ann Arbor: Center for Research Utilization of Scientific Knowledge, Institute for Social Research, the University of Michigan, 1971.

King, Donald W. *Key Papers in the Economics of Information*. White Plains, N.Y.: Knowledge Industry Publications, 1980.

Kochen, Manfred, ed. *The Growth of Knowledge: Readings in Organization and Retrieval of Information*. New York: Wiley, 1967.

Kochen, Manfred. "WISE: A World Information Synthesis and Encyclopedia." *Journal of Documentation* 28 (December 1972):322-43.

Kochen, Manfred. "Information and Society." *Annual Review of Information Science and Technology* 18 (1977):277.

Lias, E. *Future Mind: The Microcomputer--New Medium, New Mental Environment*. Boston: Little, Brown and Co., 1982.

Machlup, Fritz, and Stephen Kagan. "The Changing Structure of the Knowledge-Producing Labor Force." Paper no. 78-01. Discussion Series, New York University, Center for Applied Economics, January 1978.

McLuhan, Marshall. *Understanding Media: The Extension of Man*. New York: Bantam, 1964.

McLuhan, Marshall, and Q. Fiore. *The Medium Is the Massage*. New York: Bantam, 1967.

Marwick, Arthur. "Print, Pictures, and Sound: World War and the British Experience." *Daedalus* 3 (Fall 1982):135-56.

Poirier, Richard. "Literature, Technology, and People." *Daedalus* 3 (Fall 1982):61-74.

Rand Report. Privacy and Security in Personal Information Databand Systems. Report 1044-NSF, March 1974.

Saracevic, Tefko, ed. *Introduction to Information Science*. New York: R. R. Bowker, 1970.

Schudson, Michael. "The Politics of Narrative Form: The Emergence of News Conventions in Print and Television." *Daedalus* 3 (Fall 1982):97-112.

Smith, Anthony. "Information Technology and the Myth of Abundance." *Daedalus* 3 (Fall 1982):1-16.

Toffler, Alvin. *Future Shock*. New York: Bantam, 1970.

Toffler, Alvin. *The Third Wave*. New York: William Morrow, 1980.

UNESCO. *Multinational Exchange Mechanisms of Educational Audio-Visual Materials*. Part I: Situations and Suggestions; Part 2: Appendices. Paris: UNESCO, Center of Studies and Realizations for Permanent Education, 1976.

Weizenbaum, Joseph. *Computer Power and Human Reason: From Judgment to Calculation*. San Francisco: W. H. Freeman, 1976.

9
The Future of Information Science

Information science emerged from the need to change the way we generate, use, and transfer knowledge. Information science in the future will be shaped by the social and cultural changes that evolve from these needs. Thus, the future of information science ultimately rests on a knowledge system encompassing all segments of the human, technological, and social framework--a system capable of extending awareness to understanding, developing the means for applying knowledge, synthesizing ideas, and evaluating decisions. The future of the science also rests on the ability of professionals in business and academia to adopt new roles in the face of changing needs.

KEY ISSUES

Several important issues will influence the future development of information science:

1.   Consciousness among individuals in all walks of life of the role and importance of information and knowledge.

2. The balanced distribution of, access to, and efficient, effective use of information and knowledge resources to all mankind.

3. The application of new information technology.

Information Consciousness

The acceptance of information science as a bona fide discipline depends on the recognition of information and knowledge as important resources meriting serious study. In most areas of society there is only superficial acceptance of the importance of information and knowledge to individuals. The following, however, can be considered as signs of deeper acceptance of the importance of information as a resource, and therefore of information science:

1. The establishment by many nations of government agencies whose function is to help meet the information and knowledge requirements of their people.

2. UNESCO's massive program to improve the ability of both developed and developing nations to have access to world knowledge.

3. The creation of the National Commission of Library and Information Science established by Congress in 1970. This commission is a permanent, independent agency of the U.S. government (Public Law 91-345) to advise the president and the Congress on the nation's library and information needs and to develop and carry out policies and plans on (1) access to information, (2) improving library and information services to meet changing needs, (3) information technology and productivity, and (4) policy planning and advice (Hashim 1985).

4. A call for the U.S. legislature to establish an information policy (Chartrand 1986). The important issues are federal information resource management; information

technology for education, innovation, and competitiveness; telecommunications, broadcasting, and satellite transmission; internal communications and information policy; information disclosure, confidentiality, and the right to privacy; computer regulation and crime; intellectual property; library and archives policies; government information systems, clearinghouses, and disseminations. These bills have been introduced. It remains to be seen how many become laws.

5.   The establishment of offices and departments headed by an information manager in academic and industrial institutions to ensure the proper planning, operating, and control of information-knowledge resources (Horton 1978).

6.   The international recognition of the role that information systems can play in critical situations facing mankind. Information systems are now under consideration for earthquake prediction (Chartrand 1986), pollution control, weather analysis, and nuclear power plant control.

Balanced Distribution of Information and Knowledge

The means for establishing adequate worldwide distribution of information and knowledge rest on the analysis and design of information systems that meet the requirements of people throughout the world. People need to be aware of current events and have the knowledge to evaluate them. Human information needs are related to basic drives toward self-development and growth. They also reflect the need to meet contingencies critical to individual and group survival. The basic capabilities required to meet these needs in the future will be (1) literacy, (2) ability to acquire and operate technology, and (3) a clear understanding of how information systems function in meeting such needs (information system literacy). The future of information science rests on the ability of the science to educate individuals with a clear understanding of these requirements in the analysis and design of information systems (DeSolla Price 1963).

Applications of New Information Technology

The future of information science is also related to trends in the development of technology. Information scientists must acknowledge developments in technology and determine whether they can be integrated to achieve useful ends.

Edward Lias's (1982) analysis of technology suggests several principles that can be used to project the future of information systems and consequently the future of information science.

Pipeline Principle

Once things (in this instance information technologies) are set in motion they will produce an effect even if the forces behind that motion no longer operate.

Amalgamation of Old into New

As new technologies surface, they include the characteristics of previous technology. For example, television incorporates many aspects of motion pictures. Most information systems that exist today are not new, but rather are versions of oider systems. New technologies are integrated into older structures.

Generality to Specificity

Technology seems to move from uses that are general to those that are specific. Information systems therefore must be designed to meet the needs of large groups of people, but must have characteristics that can be assimilated and accommodated easily to fit the needs of specific users.

Displacement and Integration

Old technology will disappear unless it can be integrated within new technology. Paper and pencil are old technologies. Many scholars have speculated about the possibility of a paperless society of the future. Electronic mail could make letter writing obsolete. The computer could substantially reduce the need for a paper and pencil. Of course, old technology will not be displaced until new technology becomes widely available. We can add to Lias's fourth principle by simply saying that the importance of old technology will diminish as a function of new emerging technologies.

Principle of Self-Feeding Change

This principle states that the more things change the more they will change. During the past two decades, technological developments have created vast changes in the way we interact with each other. These changes are reflected in social values. The manner in which we conduct business, particularly in the Western world (e.g., electronic-oriented commerce), has resulted in a new perspective about how we think about ourselves and others. Based on this principle we can also expect massive changes in the way we work, learn, and play. Toffler (1970) projected a return to the home as a place of work. If realized, such a change will create corresponding changes in our work patterns.

New Directions for Professionals

Tremendous growth in the volume of recorded data, combined with increasing sophistication of information technologies, is fast overwhelming the individual who seeks to meet a specific information need. There is a growing interest in information services that go beyond the library. These services are directed to individuals or institutions whose information and knowledge needs require the special attention of an intermediary or synthesizer. Some new professional identities that are emerging in response to changing information needs are:

Information broker: Facilitates the acquisition of data and knowledge commodities (reports, books, etc.). Brokers are skilled in basic research in specialized areas.

Information consultants: These are experts in specific subject areas. They study and provide recommendations on areas of knowledge relevant to a problem or project.

Information counselors: They establish procedures to determine the information-knowledge need of a client (diagnosis), prescribe the sequence and ordering of material to meet the need (prescription), and determine the effectiveness of the diagnosis and prescription in meeting the need (evaluation). Information counseling is client-centered and approximates the role of the teacher in guiding the client to efficient and effective use of information.

THE OBLIGATION OF INFORMATION SCIENCE

Awareness of the importance of information fosters awareness of the need to distribute it equitably, to serve the needs of society as a whole and not a privileged subgroup. Information professionals must realize that, although our roles are diverse, there are commonalities in our work with which we must all be concerned.

The following statement expressed by Kochen (1981) presents an enlightened view of the future of information science.

> The future is shaped largely by entrepreneurs and innovators with the vision to bend, steer, and control the technology toward worthwhile goals. Tomorrow's entrepreneurs are stimulated and guided by those of today. They can function only if supported by executives in the knowledge industry. Somehow, we must inject the idea that the systems they will create are primarily *human* systems. That is, they must serve primarily human ends by human means. Basic human values must predominate. Man and machine are not equal partners. There is still time for persons, rather than the momentum of technological growth, to shape technology and communication in the future.

REFERENCES

Borguslaw, Robert. *The New Utopians: The Study of System Design and Social Change*. Englewood Cliffs, N.J.: Prentice-Hall, 1965.

Chartrand, Robert Lee. "Information Science for Emergency Management." *Bulletin of the American Society of Information Science* 12, no. 3 (1986):4-9, 12-13.

Deitel, Harvey, and Barbara Deitel. *Computers and Data Processing*. Orlando, Fla.: Academic Press, 1985.

DeSolla Price, P.V. "Prologue to a Science." In *Little Science Big Science*. New York: Columbia University Press, 1963, 1-32.

Garfield, Eugene, Morton V. Matlin, and Henry Small. "Citation Data as Science Indicators." In *Toward a Metric of Science: The Advent of Science Indicators*. New York: Wiley 1978.

Hashim, Elinor M. "National Committee of Library and Information Science: A Brief Overview." *JASIS*, no. 6 (November 1986) 360.

Horton, Forest Woody, Jr. "The Emerging Information Manager Professional." In *Information Science in Action: System Design*. Edited by A. Debons and A. Larson. The Hague: Martinus Nijhoff, 1978.

Kochen, Manfred. "Technology and Communication in the Future." *Journal of the American Society of Information Science* 32 (March 1981):149.

Kochen, Manfred. "WISE: A World Information Synthesis and Encyclopedia." *Journal of Documentation* 28 (December 1972).

Lias, Edward J. *Future Mind: The Microcomputer--New Medium, New Mental Environment*. Boston, Little, Brown and Co., 1982.

Logsdown, T. *The Robot Revolution*. New York: Simon and Schuster, 1984.

Lukasiewicz, J. "The Ignorance Explosion: A Contribution to the Study of Confrontation of Man with the Complexity of Science-based Society and Environment." *Transactions of the New York Academy of Science*, series 2, 1972, 34-373.

Machlup, Fritz, and Kenneth Leeson. *Information through the Printed Word: The Dissemination of Scholarly Scientific and Intellectual Knowledge*. New York: Praeger, 1980.

Martensson, Nils. "Applications of Industrial Robots, Technical and Economic Constraints. In *Robotics and Artificial Intelligence*. Edited by M. Brady, L. A. Geehardt, and H. F. Davidson. Berlin: Springer Verlag, 1984, 519-41.

Martins, Gary. "The Que-Selling of Expert Systems." *Datamation*, November 1984, 76-80.

Puzzanghera, Paul. "D.S.S. Market: Horizontal. Vertical Growth Seen." *Software News*, December 1984.

Rathswohl, Eugene J. "Tutorial, Group 1: Nature of Information." In *Perspectives in Information Science*. Leyden: Noordhoff, 1975.

Schoderbek, P. O., Charles G. Schoderbek, and Astevios G. Kefalas. *Management Systems*. 3d ed. Plano, Texas: Business Publications, 1985, 295.

Thierauf, Robert J., and George W. Reynolds. *Effective Management Information Systems: Accent on Current Practices*. Columbus, Oh.: Charles E. Merrill, 1984, 238-42.

Toffler, Alvin. *Future Shock*. New York: Random House, 1970.

White, Herbert. "Endpoint." *Bulletin of the American Society of Information Science* 11, no. 6 (1985):18-19.

Yannis, H. *Telecommunications: Trends and Directions*. Mass: The Communications Division, Electronic Industries Association, May 1981, 20-22.

Index

A

academic programs
  see education
Ackoff, Russell L., 57, 59, 60, 61, 62
analyzer, 27
artificial intelligence, 80, 130
associations, professional, 38
automation, 27

B

bandwidth, 108
Becker, Joseph, 12
behavioral science, 16
Bertelanffy, Ludwig von, 58
bibliometrist disciplines
  see documentalist disciplines
bionics, 18
Blake, M.L., 30
Borko, Harold, 11, 125
Boulding, Kenneth E., 57
brainstorming, 48
Buckland, Michael K., 138
business, 35

C

C³
  see command-control-
    communication systems
cable television, 109
case histories, 48
cellular telephone

see radio, cellular
censorship, 148
channel, defined, 92
Churchman, C. West, 58, 63, 65, 118
classification-categorization
  theory, 128
classification theory, 130
codes, 76
command-control-
  communication
  environments, 53
command-control-
  communication systems
  influence on information
    science, 10
commodity, information as, 2
communication
  awareness as effect, 104
  barriers, 150
  as discipline, 10-12
  effect of social structure, 143
  as information transfer, 2, 103
  models, 73-77
  see also information transfer
communication science, 34, 36
  skills needed for, 32-33

functions, 79-82
models, 130
publications
    journals, 12, 38, 39-40
    seminal books in
        information science, 11
    see also associations,
        professional;
        conferences,
        professional

R

radar, 89
radio, 94
    cellular, 95
remote sensing, 90
robotics, 97-98
robots, 97
routine processor of
    information, 26

S

sampling, 47
Samuelson, Kjell, 72
Saracevic, Tefko, 11, 29
satellites, 90, 94, 108
Schoderbek, P.P., 119
Scientific and Technical
    Information program, 9
Scott, George M., 79
semiautomated ground
    environment (SAGE), 10
Shannon, Claude E., 73-74, 92,
    129, 131
signal, 76
signal-detection theory, 88-89
signal transmission
    Otten's model, 76
    Shannon's model, 73

simulation, 50-53
society
    influence on, 15
    structure, 143
sonar, 89
specialists, information, 22
STI
    see Scientific and Technical
        Information program
structures
    action, 61
surveys, 46
symbol
    acquisition, 88
    defined, 5
synthesis, 115-39
    capacity, 125
    defined, 115-16
    procedure, 125
system
    abstract, 59
    characteristics, 63
    closed, 61
    concrete, 59-62
    definition, 57
    human control, 134
    living, subsystems, 66-67
    management, 77-78
    models, 63-77
    open, 61
    purposeful, 59
    types, 59
system analysis
    defined, 117, 119, 125
    factors, 124
    strategies, 118
system analysis and design,
    115-39
    goal, 116

mandates, 122-5
see also system design
system analysis procedure
   stages, 120-21
system boundaries, 59
system components
   integration, 127
   synthesis, 127
system design, 23, 43-44, 64,
     115-25, 135
   defined, 117, 125, 133
   factors, 122, 123
   see also system analysis and
     design
system dynamics, 119
system model
   Churchman's, 63
systems approach
   defined, 58
system specification
   revision, 126
systems theory, 57-84
   general, 57
systems thinking
   aspects, 118

T

Taylor, Robert S., 83
technologists, information, 22
technology
   role in human functions,
     135-37
   role in system functions, 135-
     37
telecommunications, 106
teleconferencing, 109
teleport technology, 95
telescopy, 90
theorists, information, 22

Toffler, Alvin, 152
transformer of information, 26
transmission channels, 150
transmission technology, 87-95
transmission theory, 129
transponder, 108, 109
transporter of information, 26
Trauth, Eileen More, 4

U

UNESCO, 150, 158

W

Wasserman, Paul, 28
wisdom
   defined, 6, 8
   as part of a continuum, 5, 6
world knowledge system, 149

X

xerography, 105

Y

Yovits, Marshall C., 71, 72

Z

Zimmerman, Patricia J., 123